AMERICAN ARCHITECTURE

AMERICAN ARCHITECTURE

BY

FISKE KIMBALL

ILLUSTRATED

AMS PRESS
NEW YORK

Reprinted from the edition of 1928, Indianapolis
First AMS EDITION published 1970
Manufactured in the United States of America

Library of Congress Catalog Card Number: 77-108121
SBN: 404-03676-7

AMS PRESS, INC.
New York, N. Y. 10003

CONTENTS

CHAPTER   PAGE

     FOREWORD 13

I   THE BEGINNINGS 17

II   THE AFTERGLOW OF THE MIDDLE AGES . 27

III   FROM JACOBEAN TO GEORGIAN . . . 35

IV   THE HEYDAY OF THE ENGLISH COLONIES . 41

V   PROVINCIAL TYPES OF THE SEABOARD . . 57

VI   SPANISH AND FRENCH OUTPOSTS . . . 63

VII   FIRST WORKS UNDER THE REPUBLIC . . 69

VIII   THE GREEK REVIVAL 95

IX   ROMANTICISM AND THE GOTHIC . . . 111

X   A CONFUSION OF TONGUES . . . 119

XI   THE STAGE OF MODERNISM: NEW
     MATERIALS AND NEW TYPES . . . 135

XII   WHAT IS ARCHITECTURE? THE POLES OF
     MODERNISM: FUNCTION AND FORM . . 147

XIII   THE TRIUMPH OF CLASSICAL FORM . . 171

XIV   COUNTER-CURRENTS 191

XV   THE PRESENT 203

XVI   MANHATTAN 221

     EPILOGUE 227

     NOTES 231

     INDEX 247

LIST OF ILLUSTRATIONS

FACING PAGE

"English wigwams"—types of the first shelters
in New England 20

A log house of the Swedes—Delaware County,
Pennsylvania 21

An early Anglican church—St. Luke's, Isle of
Wight County, Virginia 28

An early evangelical chapel—Muhlenberg's church
at Trappe, Pennsylvania 29

The home of a New England divine—the Parson
Capen house at Topsfield, Massachusetts . . 36

The Anglican communion—Saint Paul's chapel,
New York 37

The old State House in Philadelphia—Independence Hall 46

A Virginia gentleman's seat—Westover on the
James 47

The colonial style in flower—the Brewton portico,
Charleston 50

The colonial style in flower—the Great Chamber
at Mount Pleasant 51

A New England farmhouse—the Barker house,
Pembroke, Massachusetts 58

A Dutch farmhouse—the Rapalje house, New
Lots, Long Island 59

A Pennsylvania doorway—the Sister house at
Ephrata 60

LIST OF ILLUSTRATIONS—Continued

FACING PAGE

A Pennsylvania barn—Bucks County 61

The Spaniards in Texas—Mission San José, San Antonio 64

The Spaniards in California—Mission Santa Bárbara 65

On a Louisiana plantation—Burnside on the Mississippi 72

The first building of the Republic—the Virginia Capitol, Jefferson's model 73

The federal Capitol—Thornton's design . . . 82

France in America—the New York City Hall . 83

Rome in America—the University of Virginia . 86

An Adam interior—the oval drawing-room at Lemon Hill, Philadelphia 87

An Adam house in New England—the Lyman house at Waltham, Massachusetts 90

A house of the Piedmont—Monticello, the home of Jefferson 91

The beginnings of the Greek revival—the Bank of Pennsylvania, Latrobe's design 96

The triumph of Greek revival—the Bank of the United States, Philadelphia 97

The Greek Column—the Washington Monument in Baltimore 100

The Greek House—Andalusia on the Delaware . 101

The early Gothic revival—the Eastern Penitentiary, Philadelphia 126

Gilded reminiscences—Biltmore 127

Later Gothic—the Chapel at West Point . . . 156

LIST OF ILLUSTRATIONS—Concluded

FACING PAGE

The steel frame—the Wainwright Building, Saint Louis 157

The return to classical form—the Villard houses, New York 164

The music of surface—the Boston Public Library 165

The triumph of classical form—the Court of Honor, Chicago 182

The music of space—the Pennsylvania waiting room, New York 183

The poles of modernism: the Guaranty (Prudential) Building, Buffalo; Apartments for the Century Holding Company, New York . . . 186

Old material and new form—the Wainwright tomb, St. Louis 187

New use and new form—the Larkin Factory, Buffalo 194

New material and new form—Unity Temple, Oak Park 195

The cathedral of Mammon—Woolworth Building, New York 204

The arrow—Bush tower, New York 205

Masses—Hotel Shelton, New York 214

Mass and line—the American Radiator Building, New York 215

Mass and line—the New York Telephone Building, New York 220

The grotesque—Times Square at night . . . 221

The magic mountain—Lower Manhattan from the Bay 222

The canyon—Lower Broadway 223

FOREWORD

AMERICAN ARCHITECTURE

FOREWORD

AMONG a people with the vast material task of conquering the wilderness of a continent, mastering the riches of its soil, its forests, its waters and mountains, artistic expression takes chiefly the form of building, of architecture. It is in architecture, of all the arts, that America has said best what it has had to say. It is in architecture that America, grown to imperial might, has said something new and vital in art.

Its history has sometimes been represented as a degeneration. Under Ruskin's system of moral values, falsely imported into the field of art, the Colonial day has been glorified as a golden age of honest traditional craftsmanship, the modern vilified as false and base. We can not take this view. To us the Colonial style, with all its provincial charm, is still in leading strings. Only with the founding of the Republic does a creative spirit appear, a new sense of form. Then, as a new civilization takes shape, amid the hum of harvester and factory, a new material, steel, leaps from the earth. Its towers, rising in sunshine and storm, glowing in the night, embody the aspiration of a new world.

I

THE BEGINNINGS

CHAPTER I

THE BEGINNINGS

INTO the wilderness of virgin forest came, in the seventeenth century, English, Swedes and Dutch. A few were gentlefolk, used to the houses of brick and stone and framed timber then confined at home to their own class. The majority were yeomen, tenants, or farm laborers, coming from the "frail houses" of wattle, clay, sod and thatch, in which the rural population of Europe then had its miserable shelter. There was little in their past existence for them to miss. Glass windows and brick chimneys were luxuries to which they were not accustomed. To all but the Swedes an abundance of timber was a novelty. To the men of every country there came for the first time the boon of free land for all.

Never had there been such a leveler. In their first winter at Massachusetts Bay, Winthrop had to release his servants, who took up their own tracts. Proprietaries and grants there might be, but, with land in inexhaustible supply, these would not keep men from streaming to the frontier of ownership. From that day nearly to our own, when the public domain approaches exhaustion, this freedom of the land is the key to American development. Democracy with its far-reaching effects was rooted in the soil, and for over two hundred years only the enslavement of another race could keep men in bondage.

Colonists, be they Greeks at the Pillars of Hercules, Romans in the forests of the Rhine, or Europeans on the opposite fringe of the Atlantic, strive first to make their new home like the old. To create in a new continent a new civilization and a new art is farthest from their thoughts. All their effort is to secure, and then to hold against all the odds of difference and of distance, what they knew in the mother country at the time they left. Changes are forced on them by the new environment, to be sure, but they come against all the resistance of colonial conservatism. New England, New Netherlands, New France and New Spain were, so long as they remained colonies, as near like their mothers as filial imitation could make them.

[18]

THE BEGINNINGS

Thus at first the settlers built their houses like those they had known. The common folk at Jamestown and Plymouth made shelters with slanting poles covered with brush, reeds and earth, perhaps over a low wall of stakes and wattle plastered with clay. These were the "English wigwams" of early chroniclers—by no means like those of the Indians, as some have thought. Sometimes, as in the church at Plymouth and later in the houses of English settlers in East Jersey, sawn planks were driven into the ground to make what were called palisaded houses. In Connecticut and in Philadelphia "caves" or "cellars" were made by digging into the banks, walling and roofing with sods and brush.

The log house, of horizontal logs notched together at the corners and chinked with clay, which has been ignorantly assumed to have been borrowed from the aborigines by the first settlers, was unknown either to the Indians or to the early English colonists. It seems to have been brought in from the Continent by the Swedes of the Delaware, the first settlers from northern Europe, where it was known also by the Swiss and Germans who followed. It first commended itself to the English through its superior strength for forts and prisons: Before the end of the century "garrisons" and blockhouses of squared logs dotted the New England rivers and coasts. Prisoners could not be held in the frail shelters, and in Georgia, at first, "log house" definitely meant a jail. Obviously suited to the densely forested new country, where trees must be felled to clear the land for tillage, the log house gradually became the typical home of the later frontiersman.

Long before this, and soon after the first settlement, the governors, the ministers and the men of prominence had begun to build houses of frame, of brick and of stone, and these materials were used also for the churches. The typical better house of the rural districts and towns in England and central Europe at the beginning of the seventeenth century was what we now call the half-timbered house. It had a heavy hewn frame of oak, jointed and pinned, and filled in with "cat-and-clay" (rolls of clay and straw), with sun-dried brick, or with wattle, plastered with clay and washed with lime. Such houses were

ENGLISH WIGWAMS

Types of the first shelters in New England

A LOG HOUSE OF THE SWEDES—Delaware County, Pennsylvania

built for Endecott and Winthrop at Salem and Charlestown. Some built a century later by the Germans still survive in central Pennsylvania. Very soon, however, it was found that the severer climate of America demanded some exterior covering. The English supplied this by hanging the house with weather-boards, not uncommon then in Kent, where they survive in houses which clearly show the origin of the typical American form. The filling of the frame behind by brick or plaster long survived, although it was gradually disused, and the timber house came to have the open frame we know to-day.

Although thatched roofs survived until the end of the century, and slate and tile came into use, the characteristic roof covering was shingle. Far from being regarded in England as inferior, it was there so costly as to be restricted to church steeples where weight was a consideration. On the American coast cedar was everywhere, and shingle replaced thatch two centuries before the use of thatch was generally abandoned abroad.

By 1650 the ordinary artisan and farmer in the older colonies had a small house of frame, a story and a half in height, one room on each floor—superior perhaps to what he could have hoped for in the Old World. That wooden shutters still often served in place of glass casements, and that many chimneys remained of catted clay, was only what was usual on the same social level in Europe.

The exhaustion of the forests in England during the later seventeenth century led to the abandonment of frame construction there, and the increasing use of brick and stone by the common man, whose position had been greatly improved during the Civil Wars. In America wood remained plentiful. It was made cheaper still by sawmills, scarcely known in England, introduced from the Continent. Even until to-day, after three centuries of wanton cutting, wood has remained at an advantage in cost over brick or stone. The dampness of masonry houses, in a climate of extremes, also caused prejudice against them. Nevertheless houses and churches of brick or stone were built from an early time in those colonies where the materials were readily available. In Pennsylvania—founded near the end of the century—they formed the majority.

The crucial material for building in stone was

lime. It was lack of limestone near Tidewater that hampered the New England and Virginia colonists from building much in brick. Governor Winthrop tried building a stone house at Medford with clay mortar, but the rain washed it quickly to the ground. Oyster shells furnished the only resource, and when the Indian beds of these neared exhaustion the authorities had to forbid the use of oysters for anything but food and bait. Roger Williams had limestone at Providence Plantation and started a flourishing trade, while his people built houses exceptional for their vast chimneys of stone, filling the whole end of the house. On the Schuylkill there was abundance of lime, and the colonists, familiar with London as rebuilt after the Great Fire of 1666, used brick and the fine ledge stone which was so plentiful and so easily split.

The legend of brick brought from England, or from Holland, is repeated of almost every fine old brick building in the colonies. The records show this to be a myth, except for a few cases in New Netherlands. Brickmaking is one of the simplest of arts. Brickmakers came with the first settlers. Clay and wood to burn it were abundant. It would seem as if any one who had seen the soil of the Tidewater would realize that importing brick was bringing coals to Newcastle.

II

THE AFTERGLOW OF THE MIDDLE AGES

CHAPTER II

THE AFTERGLOW OF THE MIDDLE AGES

In the first buildings of frame and of masonry, indeed in all those constructed down to the end of the seventeenth century, we see a survival of the art of the Middle Ages. Steep roofs, leaded casements, clustered chimney-stacks and exposed construction, the most striking features of these buildings, all had come down from the Gothic. They had persisted in the great noble houses of Elizabethan and Jacobean England, and were a greater part of their effect than the new Italian adornments of the classic orders. In the churches and the small houses of England, the Italian influence had not yet been felt at all when the first colonists set sail. In rural England and in Germany the peasant and ordinary dweller of the rural town built on for generations after this in the spirit of the Middle Ages. It is not surprising that in America, on the extreme outskirt of European civilization,

[27]

the Renaissance should have been long in making itself felt. Even for the rich, even for the gentlemen who came, the decent satisfaction of needs was long all that could be secured. Under these conditions the Gothic stock of north European art flourished on here for a long time before receiving the grafts from the south.

The churches were the first fruits of common effort, whether in the Biblical communities of New England where town and parish were one, or among the dispersed plantation parishes of Virginia. In both, the Gothic forms were used, but the type of edifice for the established Church of England differed markedly from that of the more extreme Protestant cults, in accordance with their models in the Old World.

The Anglican church-building of Virginia was merely a rural English parish church of its time, built across the water. The earliest, still surviving in part, was the one at Jamestown. A large square tower stood before a buttressed nave. In Saint Luke's Church, built on the same model near by in Isle of Wight, we see the details of the upbuilding: a steep roof with stepped gable and pointed Gothic windows divided by

Photograph by H. P. Cook

AN EARLY ANGLICAN CHURCH
St. Luke's, Isle of Wight County, Virginia

Courtesy of the Pennsylvania Museum

AN EARLY EVANGELICAL CHAPEL

Muhlenberg's Church at Trappe, Pennsylvania

tracery of brick. Only in the square blocks at the corners of the tower, and in the triangle above the door—faint suggestion of the temple front—do we find the first hints of classic influence. Trinity Church, New York, built within the eighteenth century and burned in the Revolution, was still Gothic in its form, as were the stone churches of the Dutch in New Jersey, and the Welsh chapel of Saint David's at Radnor in Pennsylvania.

The New England meeting-house was a dissenting chapel of the kind which came into being at the very beginnings of Protestantism, with Luther. English examples are little known, but they exist, and show all essentials of the scheme: a broad hall with galleries on three sides, the high pulpit on the fourth long wall opposite the entrance porch. The earliest which survives in the Colonies, the "Old Ship" at Hingham, still shows amid modern gimcracks the curved braces which gave it its name. No unspoiled church interior of this early character survives in New England, but one in which it persisted long after 1700 may be seen in Muhlenberg's church at Trappe in Pennsylvania, the cradle of the American Lutheran communion. Here one may still find the box-pews, the rough tiers of gallery benches, the posts and rails of a character which in England would be called Jacobean. According to the Lutheran ritual the sanctuary is here at one end of the church, with the altar in the center, the high pulpit at one side.

The timber houses of the seventeenth century survive in numbers in New England. Originally they were but a single room in depth, one or two rooms long, at most two stories and a half in height. Their great oak and pine frames are elaborately jointed, and richly beveled and molded to form also the chief decorative element. In the more ambitious houses, as in the medieval houses of Europe, the upper story overhung the lower, with moldings or pendants hewn on the frame. Banks of hinged casements with small square or diamond-shaped leaded panes pierced the broad surfaces of weather-boards. Exactness of symmetry was little regarded: the spacing followed the unequal size of rooms behind, after the frank practise of the Middle Ages. Inside, the cavernous fireplace, spanned by a great beam, was the focus of family life. The partitions and sometimes also the outer walls of the rooms were wainscoted with broad boards molded at the joints.

In the brick houses the most striking features were the tall chimney-stacks which rose at the gable-ends, sometimes with a cluster of separate flues and with the gable itself stepped and curved, as in the Jacobean houses of England. Bacon's Castle in Virginia now gives the best idea of the type, which was illustrated also in the great house of Peter Sergeant in Boston (later the Province House), and at Medway and Middleton in Carolina. The addition of a porch in front and stairs at the rear might make the house in the form of a cross, as at Bacon's Castle; or it might have its plan in the shape of H or E, surviving from the time of Elizabeth, as at Fairfield, Virginia, and the first City Hall in New York. Long afterward indeed, the type persisted in Tuckahoe, home of the Randolphs, in Stratford, home of the Lees, and in Browne's Folly at Beverly, Massachusetts. At the Mulberry in Carolina there were even four corner towers.

III

FROM JACOBEAN TO GEORGIAN

CHAPTER III

FROM JACOBEAN TO GEORGIAN

THE first considerable use of the newer classical or academic forms in English architecture was in the rebuilding of London after the Great Fire of 1666; their first considerable adoption in America followed the founding of Philadelphia by William Penn in 1682. Even here leaded casements, the most obvious of survivals from the earlier day, were used at first, but in the same buildings there appeared the signs of change. These expressed both the practical trend to larger accommodations with greater convenience and privacy, and the artistic tendency from the nervous emphasis of the Gothic with its revealed structure, to the calm of the classic with its abstract decorative form.

Some characteristic changes were the doubling of the rooms to make deeper, four-square plans, the raising of the stories, the flattening of the roofs and the cutting of their upper slopes to form the "gambrel," the tendency to abandon the gable and have a level cornice all about, the placing of a molded chimneypiece about the fireplace. The little house built, before his arrival, for William Penn himself was perhaps the first to show many of these. With the opening of the new century they gradually became common everywhere. Then, too, the sash window with wooden bars, sliding up and down as we know it, was adopted. Paneling replaced sheathing in the wainscot of the interior.

Thus came into being the fine early Georgian house of the seventeen-twenties, as we find it in the McPhædris house at Portsmouth, the Robert Brewton house at Charleston, at Shirley in Virginia, at Stenton and Hope Lodge and Cedar Grove near Philadelphia. As yet there was no rich doorway, like the one from a later generation at the McPhædris house, no portico like the one added a century afterward at Shirley. All was quietude, simplicity. The bold line of the cornice with its brackets broke the clear sunlight on walls which derive their chief or only ornament from the sober ordered windows with small panes, broad frames and bars. Inside the treat-

Courtesy of the Topsfield Historical Society

THE HOME OF A NEW ENGLAND DIVINE

The Parson Capen house at Topsfield, Massachusetts

THE ANGLICAN COMMUNION
Saint Paul's Chapel, New York

ment was simple, with bold projecting moldings
and panels, but with little use as yet of pilasters
or the richer classic elements.

In the same vein of simplicity were the typical
churches of the time: the Old South and Christ
Church in Boston, Bruton Church at Williamsburg and Christ Church in Lancaster County,
Virginia, St. Paul's at Edenton in Carolina, all
of mellow brick; the Tennent Church at Freehold, New Jersey,—cradle of Presbyterianism in
America,—of white shingle.

The early college buildings at Harvard, William and Mary, and Yale were not more elaborate, although for William and Mary Sir Christopher Wren seems to have sent a design from
London, the only real one of his in the Colonies,
where so many buildings have a legend of his
authorship. Essentially they were barracks of
fine brickwork—justifying, in spite of their
pleasant texture, Jefferson's scornful later com-
ment that "but that they have roofs, they might
be mistaken for brick kilns."

IV

THE HEYDAY OF THE ENGLISH COLONIES

CHAPTER IV

THE HEYDAY OF THE ENGLISH COLONIES

THE Colonial style came to flower in the fifty years before the Revolution. This was a period of rich doorways, of Palladian windows, of tall pilasters, of porticoes rising one on another, of elaborate mantels and overmantels, of carved staircases, of ornamented ceilings.

The Tidewater planters of Virginia and Maryland and Carolina, the patroons of the Hudson, the merchants of Philadelphia and New York, of Boston and Salem and Portsmouth had accumulated wealth. They lavished it on houses which were luxurious, if small judged by foreign standards. The Anglican Church was now well supported in the provincial capitals; philanthropy began the founding of hospitals and libraries; the colonial assemblies, with their growing power, housed themselves worthily for the first time.

The more ambitious models of Jones and

[41]

Wren and their followers in England now began to be observed. Jones' style, "solid, proportionable according to rule, masculine and unaffected," lay at the base. Wren had brought to this more of the movement and fancy of the southern baroque, had made it less severe, more intimate. The forms of detail were broken and interwoven, the graceful opposed curves of the swan-neck appeared in the crown of doorways and chimneypieces.

The new forms were derived in America less from any great influx of fresh craftsmen, who came in but small numbers, than from books. The academic system of the eighteenth century was codified in books with a simplicity and precision which have never been rivaled. As fast as they appeared, these books brought to America every new phase of building fashion, from the heavy Palladian style of the followers of Jones to the gay French and Chinese fantasies of Chippendale. Architecture then formed part of the education and interest of the gentleman. The owner could indicate, in these books, his preferences for the general scheme, as the competent workman—in Philadelphia some member of the

Carpenter's Company—could derive from them the details of his moldings and proportions.

The absence of any body of professional architects was thus not serious. Even in England they were rare. Only one of reputation, John James of Greenwich, seems to have crossed the sea for a brief period. Carter Burwell and Governor Tryon brought English master workmen, but even these were exceptional. In general the design was given by some gentleman of taste. The colonial governors, fresh from England, were several times laid under contribution, like Alexander Spotswood for Bruton Church and Sir Francis Bernard for Harvard Hall. The painter Smibert turned his hand to architecture for Faneuil Hall in Boston. The prince of the colonial amateurs was Peter Harrison of Newport, a gentleman whose talents were in demand far from home, and who took his reward in votes of thanks and pieces of plate. His buildings set a new standard of classical dignity and correctness. At the very end of the period Thomas Jefferson, in devouring his books, gave to Palladio the closest reading he had yet received.

Finest of the churches were those of the established communion in the seaboard towns, modeled on the new London churches by Wren and Gibbs. Charleston and Philadelphia took the lead. Saint Philip's had three tall porticoes about the steeple and western porch. Christ Church, by John Kearsley, a gentleman-amateur, had for the first time long rows of tall interior columns like Saint Bride's in London, and an external treatment of arches framed by an order. The fine tower was added later by Robert Smith, head of the Carpenter's Company. Boston followed with King's Chapel, its interior remarkable for great double columns. It was the work of Harrison, who also designed Christ Church in Cambridge, of rich sobriety, and the fine synagogue in Newport. Saint Michael's in Charleston out-rivaled its older neighbor by a still finer portico and richer steeple, after one of Gibb's published designs. In New York a Scotch builder, one MacBean, surpassed all the others with the vaulted interior of Saint Paul's Chapel and its great portico toward Broadway. In such churches the tables of the law, the high six-sided pulpits with their suspended sounding boards, were lavishly adorned with pilasters and panels.

The dissenting meeting-houses reflected some of this new splendor. Although the Puritan plan with the pulpit on the long side survived in retired towns down to the Revolution the tendency was now to adopt the more traditional plan. The front was adorned with pilasters. The steeple became universal. The light open belfry of columns, modeled on the early one of the Old South, was still used in the Connecticut Valley, as at Farmington, down to the close of the period. In the First Baptist Church at Providence, however, when it was rebuilt on the very eve of the war, the cultivated amateur, Joseph Brown, closely patterned it on the famous London steeple of St-Martin-in-the-Fields'.

Public buildings had begun about 1700 with the old State House in Boston, the old City Hall in New York, still half Jacobean, and the old Capitol at Williamsburg, in which a crude portico in two stories was attempted. A generation later, Andrew Hamilton, Speaker of the House, gave a design for the State House in Philadelphia, later to become famous as Independence Hall, which was of full Georgian character. On the exterior there were straight-forward brickwork and classical details without any attempt at academic grandeur. Inside, however, during the score of years the finishing was in progress, were created some of the most ambitious of the Colonial effects, an arched and columned hall and a vast stairway. Faneuil Hall, like Christ Church, had ordered arches in distant reminiscence of the Roman basilicas and the Colosseum. Peter Harrison came well abreast of the time abroad when he built, about the middle of the century, the Redwood Library and the Market or Town House at Newport. The Library was a little English garden temple, with portico and wings, very sedately monumental. The Market had a range of tall uniform pilasters through its two upper stories, above an open arcade. It was the motive, in little, of old Somerset House in London. In spite of its scholarly derivation, Harrison's work does not smell of the lamp. Repose and suavity of proportion, a musical harmony, make it live and give it a distinction unique in the Colonial work.

In the finer houses which reflected current fashion there was the same striving for abun-

THE OLD STATE HOUSE, PHILADELPHIA—Independence Hall

Photograph by H. P. Cook

A VIRGINIA GENTLEMAN'S SEAT

Westover on the James

dance and dignity through the ordered array of line, surface, mass and space.

The plans tended now to become wholly symmetrical. The house of four rooms to a floor, with stair hall running through from front to back, was the commonest of types, but in the finer houses, outside of New England, it was not unusual to have a great entrance hall free from stairs. This was the case with the Van Rensselaer manor house, with Mount Pleasant, Whitehall and Mount Airy. Other elements than the rectangle were rare in Colonial plans, the octagonal bay or room being the only variant. Some care for more complex effects of interior space was shown by the screens of columns in the halls at Cliveden and at the Chase house in Annapolis.

On the exterior there was at first an elaboration of individual elements. A rich door focused attention, as at Westover on the James. The corners of the house were adorned with rustic blocks, the principal windows surrounded by broken frames of columns or pilasters, as in the great Hancock house in Boston, of squared stone. When Isaac Royall raised his fine house at Medford to three stories, he even framed all the windows of the front.

Soon there came a plastic enrichment of the mass, through a central projection or pavilion with its own gable, as at Rosewell, Mount Pleasant and many other houses.

Most characteristic, however, was an adornment by the stately forms of the five orders. These might be merely isolated trophies of the fashion and classical cultivation of the builder, like those framing the front of the Royall house or the pavilion of the Hooper house in Danvers, which Lord Howe once chose as his headquarters. With greater knowledge they might form part of some more general treatment, like the proud row along the front of Governor Shirley's house in Roxbury, or the fourfold frontispiece of the lost Pinckney house in Charleston.

For the fullest ·effect there was a portico of columns standing free. It ranged from the little shelter of two columns over the door to the great porch, four columns in width and two in height, which won for John Drayton's solid Carolina house the extravagant name of Drayton's palace. Miles Brewton's great house in

Charleston and Governor John Penn's vanished mansion, Lansdowne, owed their unusual magnificence to similar two-story porticoes; and Jefferson projected one, more chaste in proportion, in his building plans for Monticello at the same period, on the eve of the Revolution.

The portico embracing both stories in a single flight of taller columns, which we tend to think of as the most characteristic Colonial feature, was scarcely applied to houses until after the Revolution. It was only Colonel Roger Morris of New York, in the fine mansion still redolent with later memories of Madame Jumel and Aaron Burr, who took, before the war, this final step in Colonial grandeur.

Most striking of the single features was the doorway. Flanked by pilasters or columns, and crowned by its little gable of triangle, segment or scroll in infinite variety, it gave the accent to the plainest front. As the Revolution approached and arched doors became common, the fanlight appeared above, its tracery of wood still massive, in harmony with the solidity of the style.

In the interior too there blossomed the abundant flowers of classical ornament. The panel-

[49]

ing was divided by pilasters which flanked the chimney-breast and the arches of hallway and alcove. Doors, windows and cupboards were set in tabernacles of molding, bracket, gable and shell. The fireplace was more richly framed, although a mantel-shelf was still often lacking, and columns appeared by the sides only in the imported chimneypieces of marble. Above, a panel was elaborately bordered and crowned. This decoration reached its apogee in such rooms as the drawing-room of the Brewton house, with its fine proportions, its coved ceiling, its broad panels from dado to cornice, its doorways, chimneypiece and portraits, reminiscent of those of Jones' splendid Double Cube at Wilton, justly thought the finest room in England.

The stairs were given an important place and lavishly ornamented. Brackets at the ends of the steps were scrolled and carved, balusters were turned with moldings and spirals. The Hancock house, with three different varieties of spiral balusters on each step, set a new fashion much followed in New England. Its newel, a *tour de force* of one spiral within another, oppositely winding, was likewise imitated for a generation.

THE COLONIAL STYLE IN FLOWER

The Brewton portico, Charleston

THE COLONIAL STYLE IN FLOWER

The Great Chamber at Mount Pleasant

Farther south it was commoner to carry the balusters themselves about the newel, beneath the hand-rail ending in a scroll.

A final touch of gaiety was added in the last houses before the Revolution by the fantastic shell work, derived from the French style of Louis XV, which came from England along with the Chippendale style in furniture. The French, the Gothic and the Chinese "tastes" were artlessly mingled without incongruity in this playful ornament. Leafage curled through shells in the scrolls flanking the fireplace of the Brice house at Annapolis; Chinese frets and carved friezes ran about the base, the dado, and the cornice of the Philadelphia mansions; the overmantel threw up a spray of curving fronds. In the panels of the mantels the animals of Æsop enacted their fables within their borders of tattered shell.

The ceilings, too, now bore their part in the beauty of the interior. At Belmont in Philadelphia the molded plaster, still heavy with reminiscences of Louis XIV, shows coats of arms and instruments of music. At Westover on the James, at Charleston in the Brewton and Huger

houses, at Philadelphia in the Powel parlor, at
Yonkers in the Philipse Manor, the moldings
disappear and the delicate foliage and shell work
itself makes an airy pattern. On the eve of the
Revolution, at Annapolis and at Kenmore in
Virginia, the scrolls again vanish in favor of the
rosettes and festoons which announce the reaction to a more severe classic ornamentation,
which was to triumph in the Adam style after
the war.

In all these finer houses we search in vain for
a note of fundamental difference from English
style. The absence of country palaces like those
of the English nobility can not obscure the equiv-
alence of the American houses with those of the
smaller English gentry of the day. The delay
and compromise in the adoption of newer architectural fashions of the metropolis was not
greater than in provincial England. In New
England, to be sure, the greater survival of wood
gave a different balance between the prevailing
materials, but elsewhere the majority of the
finest Colonial houses were of masonry. Even
in New England, where later, as in England, the
influence of the Adam style was to bring more

slender proportions and greater delicacy, more suited to execution in wood, no such change took place within the Colonial period. The heavy classic proportions still ruled. The ideal of the Colonial style remained always: conformity to current English usage.

V

PROVINCIAL TYPES OF THE SEABOARD

CHAPTER V

PROVINCIAL TYPES OF THE SEABOARD

IT WAS in the houses of the by-roads, the
simple farmsteads lagging behind the march of
progress, that characteristic local types differing from those of England gradually developed.
In these isolated regions the workmen, instead of
piquing themselves on a perfect following of the
latest London fashion, built forward unconsciously in new directions. These buildings are
more racily American, springing from the very
soil of their own colony and district.

The New England farmhouse long preserved
the lean-to which it inherited from the seventeenth century. The unbroken slope of roof
toward the north was well suited to the severe
winter, celebrated in Whittier's *Snow-Bound*.
The sheds and barns extended from it in continuous endless range. A vast central chimney
anchored the house against the sweep of the
storms. In the Plymouth Colony, on Cape Cod

and on the island of Nantucket, shingles were used for the walls as well as for the roof. Elsewhere clapboards, perhaps graded in width, formed the familiar wall covering. In the Connecticut Valley the doorway with pilasters and opposite broken scrolls, a reminiscence of the Hancock house, for which the stone had been cut at Middletown, had a special vogue. The detail, half remembered, was repeated with the quaint grammar of dialect.

About New York, extending in East Jersey and on Long Island, a different type prevailed— the so-called Dutch Colonial. The simplest houses of the Dutch under English rule, as we see them up the Hudson at Hurley and New Palz, were of whitewashed stone with steep chimneyed gables and little projection at the eaves. The better farmhouses, two rooms in depth, came to have a roof of lower slope, with a very wide overhang at front and back. Already before the Revolution it had become customary to extend this still farther, and support the front on posts to form a porch called the piazza. The painter Copley, visiting New York just before the War of Independence, found these a novelty

Courtesy of the Metropolitan Museum of Art

A NEW ENGLAND FARMHOUSE

The Barker house, Pembroke, Massachusetts

A DUTCH FARMHOUSE

The Rapalje house, New Lots, Long Island

and was the first to introduce them to New England. The gambrel roof, rare in most of the provinces of Holland, was taken up in New York as in the other English Colonies, but assumed a special form with a lower angle. The red Bergen sandstone, the long shingles, helped to give a strong local flavor.

In Pennsylvania the pervasive ledge stone gave a common element to the farmhouses of the English, the Welsh, and the Germans. As the eaves of the Dutch houses of New York overhung the walls, the broad hood at the second floor of the houses at Germantown sheltered those of the lower story.

In German counties like Berks, Lebanon and Lancaster, the language and art alike remained those of the old country. Interiors like those of the Muller house at Millbach, with fanciful raised panels, square balusters and richly wrought hinges, preserve much of the savor of the Rhineland. At Ephrata, the stronghold of the Dunkards, are monastic buildings of catted timber covered with stucco, tall-roofed and many-dormered. Most striking perhaps of all the Pennsylvania buildings are the great barns with their massive walls of stone, their sides, "overshot" to shelter the animals, supported on massive white-washed pillars.

In the South the absence of a middle class left little between the mansions and the humble quarters of the blacks. The minor plantation houses clung to the older type of steep gable roof with end chimneys. The mild climate permitted the kitchen to be in a detached building, forming with the smoke-house, dovecot and other outbuildings, a picturesque group.

These were Americanisms, differing from the King's English, as did the dialects of English districts themselves. They gave the Colonial utterance a tang of its own, without contributing anything fundamental to the common stock of European civilization. An independent initiative in architectural style, destined to have, in the sequel, far-reaching consequences, appeared only after the Revolution.

Photograph by Lewis L. Emmert

A PENNSYLVANIA DOORWAY
The Sister House at Ephrata

A PENNSYLVANIA BARN
Buck's County

VI

SPANISH AND FRENCH OUTPOSTS

CHAPTER VI

SPANISH AND FRENCH OUTPOSTS

On the borders of the Gulf, along the Rio Grande, on the shores of the Pacific, outposts of Spain and of France were built in the Latin tradition, already a century old in America before the founding of Plymouth.

At St. Augustine the Governor's House with its high stuccoed wall, its tile roof and hanging balcony, the Cathedral with its pierced belfry, its rich doorway against the whitewashed front, spoke the language of the Spanish Mediterranean.

In Texas, in New Mexico, in Arizona, the Spanish Jesuits, from the end of the sixteenth century, were founding missions. They built in the manner of the Indians, of adobe and of sundried brick, with flat roofs of clay on crude wooden beams projecting through the walls. For a century the forms were of the simplest, as in the barn-like Chapel of San José at Laguna.

Doors and windows had not yet the simplest frame. Only the pierced belfry and the Cross marked the purpose of the building on the exterior. Inside, as we still see at Chimayo, carved brackets for the roof-beams recalled the Renaissance in Spain, while in the painted altars and railings the Indian artist mingled his gay coloring. In the eighteenth-century churches, rich baroque carving was lavished on the windows and the altars. The fronts of San Xavier del Bac in Arizona, of the missions at San Antonio, had a profusion of columns and arches, of niches and scrolls. Ornate belfries rose over great towers, vaults and domes spanned the interior.

With the expulsion of the Jesuits, the task of colonizing California fell to the Franciscans. Up the coast they marched in the last years of the eighteenth century and the first of the nineteenth. A chain of missions stretched from San Diego to San Francisco and even north of the Bay. The primitive background, the ascetic traditions of the Franciscans and the dying fire of the baroque conspired to make them of great austerity. Broad walls with massive buttresses,

Courtesy of I. T. Frary

THE SPANIARDS IN TEXAS
Mission San José, San Antonio

The Spaniards in California—Mission Santa Bárbara

arched corridors and cloisters with supports
heavily square, beamed or vaulted naves, curved
gables and belfries, were the few and simple
elements, variously combined in groups of mov-
ing simplicity and beauty. The great buttressed
flank of San Gabriel, the ruined arcades of San
Juan Capistrano, the sober front of Santa
Bárbara against its background of mountains,
brand themselves deeply on memory and imagination.

The few civil buildings of the Spanish Southwest are even more unassuming. The Palace at
Santa Fé is of the simplest adobe with clay roof.
The houses of the Estudillo at San Diego, of the
De la Guerra at Santa Bárbara, the Rancho
Camulos, with their white walls, tile roofs and
green patios, are the chief. They are enough,
however, to have had across a century an
influence abidingly felt.

In New Orleans on the Mississippi it was the
French who made the beginnings. French were
the long windows opening on iron balconies,
French the rustic blocks of the Archbishop's
palace. The Spaniards came, and after the
great fire of 1788 rebuilt the Place d'Armes in

ordered arcades. Latin, New Orleans was to remain, even when it fell before the triumphant advance of the young American Republic.

VII

FIRST WORKS UNDER THE
REPUBLIC

CHAPTER VII

FIRST WORKS UNDER THE REPUBLIC

It was with the founding of the Republic that America came of age. The new political order had far-reaching consequences. It called into being governmental buildings which were not only more important than those of the Colonies hitherto, but were of types radically new in the modern world. In all classes of buildings connected with political and social institutions, the democratic and humanitarian ideals of America brought into being arrangements very different from those which were traditional in Europe. Republican institutions gave a new significance and a new form to the buildings for the legislative assemblies of the novel republican states and of the great nation soon to be welded from them.

Most vital, however, was the very fact of independence itself. The fathers of the Republic were eager to throw off provincial dependence in other matters than that of sovereignty, to get

[69]

rid of colonialism, of foreign authority. They wanted to do this even in language. Noah Webster, in his dictionary, sought to codify American usage. They wanted to do it also in art. The leader of the movement was Jefferson, the author of the Declaration of Independence itself. He hoped to make an artistic declaration of independence as well.

In his own final judgment, witnessed by his epitaph, he appears above all as a lover of freedom, whether in politics, in religion or in science; but the freedom thus loved from youth was essentially the freedom of reason to reach its own conclusions, not freedom to degenerate into formless anarchy. Trained in the law, he demanded logical system in thought. He insisted, too, on going to the sources in every field: in his fundamental study of the common law, in his researches among fossils, in his Biblical criticism. He sought the earliest precedents, among the Anglo-Saxons, the Greeks, the Romans. Hence the paradox that Jefferson, the apostle of individualism, should have chosen as his first master in architecture, Palladio, who passes as the chief representative of dogmatic authority. The

reconciliation lies first in the character of rea-
soned law borne by Palladio's architectural
system. However artificial it may seem to us, it
had in common with nature this supposed law-
fulness and reasonableness, which was doubtless
what Palladio himself felt when he wrote:
"Architecture, the imitator of Nature." Here
was the relation to natural law, one of Jefferson's
fundamental conceptions. With the weight of
primitive and classic precedent which Palladio
sought to adduce and Jefferson has been quick
to respect, the preponderance of spiritual agree-
ment between them had been overwhelming.

Jefferson now turned to the ancients, to the
Greeks and Romans whose republics then, in the
freshness of modern republicanism, seemed very
near. He hoped to secure the respect of foreign-
ers, without copying them, to be at once novel
and correct.

He had excellent preparation for the task
which his political career as Governor of Virginia, Secretary of State and President gave him
enviable power to accomplish. With the best
private library of architecture in the Colonies, he
had already made himself a competent designer

before the Revolution. While the war still raged he proposed rebuilding the Governor's Palace at Williamsburg on the lines of a classic temple, with fronts of eight columns; and, when the capital was moved to Richmond, suggested modeling the Governor's house there on Palladio's Villa Rotonda with its dome and porticoes. Immediately afterward he went to Paris for five years as American Minister, and traveled extensively in France, England, the Low Countries, Germany and Italy. His account books show that no month passed, scarcely a day passed, without his systematically visiting the buildings. What attracted him chiefly were the Roman monuments and their adaptations in the France of the hour. At Nîmes, as he wrote the Comtesse de Tessé, he gazed "whole hours at the Maison Quarrée, like a lover at his mistress"; in Paris he was "violently smitten with the Hôtel de Salm, and used to go to the Tuileries almost daily to look at it"; in southern France he was "immersed in antiquities from morning to night." "For me," he wrote, "the city of Rome is actually existing in all the splendor of its empire."

His chance to turn the architecture of his

On a Louisiana Plantation—Burnside on the Mississippi

THE FIRST BUILDING OF THE REPUBLIC

The Virginia Capitol, Jefferson's model

country into a new channel came, while he was in Paris, with the building of the Virginia Capitol at Richmond. He saw in this "a favorable opportunity of introducing into the State an example of architecture in the classic style of antiquity." Not content merely with the use of classic elements, he proposed a veritable reproduction of one of the most famous antique buildings—the temple at Nîmes known as the Maison Carrée. The interior was divided to give rooms for the assemblies and the courts, the wall pierced with windows, but the general form and proportions remained unchanged. The vast portico was united with the mass by an unbroken cornice. The simple and crystalline cubical form, the colossal scale of the columns, gave the building a novel dignity expressive of the majesty of the sovereign state. The portico was a frontispiece to all Virginia.

It has been little realized that the design long preceded anything similar abroad. The classic revival was indeed a movement which already had its beginnings there and which there also had the same ultimate ideal—the temple. Classic examples had already been imitated abroad in garden temples and commemorative monuments, but never on any such large scale and never in a building intended for practical use. The conservatism and logic of the architects rebelled. Even in England, the leader in the classical movement, although Greek details began to appear as early as 1760, the temple form was not adopted bodily for any monumental building before 1830. The Virginia Capitol preceded the Madeleine in Paris, first of the great European temple reproductions, by more than a score of years. Jefferson's insistence on the support of antique authority in the Republic anticipated the attempt of Napoleon to gain the same sanction for his own empire. In the classical movement America was thus not merely a follower—rather, a leader in pressing it to its extreme consequences.

Although the design was but crudely carried out, the building deeply stirred the American imagination. Robert Mills, a master of the next generation, wrote: "I remember the impression it made on my mind when first I came in view of it coming from the South. It gave me an idea of the effect of those Greek temples which are the admiration of the world."

FIRST WORKS UNDER REPUBLIC

The classical ideal thus embodied was ultimately to rule in America to a degree unknown in Europe, but a generation passed before its sway became universal. Leopardi has well described how the man of genius takes ten steps forward—too far for the crowd to follow. Only when lesser men have taken a single step in that direction will the multitude go with them, and so step by step finally reach the goal.

The rank and file of craftsmen long continued to work in the style of their fathers. The New England country churches like those of Lenox and Bennington, the simple farmhouses, were untouched by any breath of innovation. The ideas of church builders for a long time did not go beyond the London steeples and porticoes of Gibbs. Many of the finest houses built in the years just after the Revolution, such as the Joseph Brown house in Providence, the John Reynolds (Morris) house in Philadelphia, show nothing fundamentally novel. It is works like these which have caused buildings erected even after 1800 to be called "Colonial," and to merit the name of post-Colonial.

Meanwhile many buildings began to show a

larger dignity and a more classical character. These qualities appear first in the public buildings in which the other states and the new nation, following the lead of Virginia, housed their governments. Not merely new capitols, but whole new capitals, had to be built. The up-country men, like Jefferson, were demanding the removal of the seats of government inland from the old seaboard towns. New towns, more central, were decreed at the falls of the rivers: Richmond in Virginia, for which Jefferson gave a gridiron plan; Columbia in South Carolina; Washington, the Federal City, on the Potomac.

For the inauguration of the federal government, New York undertook an ambitious remodeling of its old City Hall. The direction of the work was entrusted to a French Major of Engineers, Pierre Charles L'Enfant. He had fought gallantly through the Revolution, and had already given proof of his artistic gifts by designing the altar-piece and choir rail of St. Paul's Chapel in the florid French style of Louis XV. In the Federal Hall he achieved a studied elegance new to those who saw it. A tall open portico with sculptured gable, raised a

story above the street, provided the setting for
Washington's oath of office, and was deeply im-
pressed on spectators of the solemn ceremony.

Among the crowd of onlookers was Charles
Bulfinch, a young gentleman of Boston, whose
easy circumstances had permitted him to make
the grand tour of Europe. He had seen the
monuments of Paris under the suggestions of
Jefferson and had retraced his route in the
South, pressing on to Rome. He brought back
from New York to Boston a drawing of the
Federal Hall, which, published in the *Massachusetts Magazine* and widely copied, served as the
model for the capitol of South Carolina. This
was the work of James Hoban, a young Irish-
man who had won a medal in the architectural
school of the Dublin Society, and had worked on
the Royal Exchange and Custom House in
Dublin.

Bulfinch himself had already submitted a design for a State House in Boston. He now
testified to his classical enthusiasm by a Roman
column on Beacon Hill and a triumphal arch for
Washington's reception in Boston. When the
State House came to execution in 1795 he gave

it the arched and colonnaded portico of the Garde-meuble in the Place de la Concorde, and crowned it with the dome, later gilded, which served the Bostonians of Oliver Wendell Holmes as "the hub of the universe."

For the projected Federal City, L'Enfant was employed to make the plans. Like all his undertakings, it was conceived on a vast scale, more suited to the ultimate growth of the country than to its actual means. He took as his model the capital of his native country, America's ally. Versailles had given the very suggestion for the founding of new capitals in the wilderness, apart from the turbulence of old centers—for St. Petersburg, Karlsruhe, and a host of others. The city of the Sun King was now to give the pattern for the seat of the republican government. The Capitol occupied the place of the palace; the President's House, of the Trianon; the Mall, of the park. From the chief centers radiate the principal avenues, giving as L'Enfant said, "a reciprocity of sight" across the gridiron of minor streets. It was a grandiose conception, a "city of magnificent distances," which has taken a century to come into its own.

"When it is proposed to prepare plans for the Capitol," Jefferson wrote to L'Enfant, "I should prefer the adoption of some one of the models of antiquity which have had the approbation of thousands of years; and for the President's house I should prefer the celebrated fronts of modern buildings, which have already received the approbation of all good judges. Such are the Gallerie du Louvre, the Garde meubles, and the two fronts of the Hôtel de Salm." At the instance of one of the Commissioners of the Federal City, L'Enfant asked for the plans of the Virginia Capitol, but they were lost in the catastrophe which followed.

L'Enfant's vaulting ambition and insubordination to all authority justified Jefferson's prophecy, years before, that a superintendent from Paris would consider himself "the Superintendent of the Directors themselves, and probably of the Government of the state also." For the designs of the federal buildings the authorities had to look elsewhere. Jefferson proposed a competition on the lines of those he had known in France. He drafted the requirements for the Capitol and the President's House, and when at first it seemed that no worthy plans would be submitted, himself sent in a design for the latter, modeled on his favorite Villa Rotonda. In the end a host of builders and amateurs competed. For the President's house a project by Hoban, following one of Gibbs' English engraved designs, with some reminiscences of Leinster House in his native Dublin, carried the day.

For the Capitol, the ablest of the competitors was Stephen Hallet, the first highly trained, professional architect to come to America. He was an *architect expert juré du roi,* who had crossed the Atlantic as a professor in a chimerical Franco-American academy of the fine arts, and had been left stranded by the French Revolution. In his first design for the Capitol he created the type with a tall central dome and wings for the two chambers, the scheme which was ultimately to be adopted almost universally for American legislative buildings. Jefferson persuaded him to send in, instead, a temple scheme with colonnades all about, and this was preferred among the designs first submitted. Hallet was retained as superintendent, and made further studies in

which he returned to the dome, but none quite
satisfied the authorities.

At this juncture there appeared on the scene
a gifted amateur, William Thornton, who was to
wage many a battle against the professionals before they finally mastered the field. "He was a
scholar and a gentleman," wrote a contemporary, "full of talent and eccentricity—a Quaker
by profession, a painter, a poet, and a horse
racer—well acquainted with the mechanic arts."
Born in the West Indies, he spent his boyhood
in England, became a Doctor of Medicine at
Edinburgh, spent some time on the Continent,
and came to America about the time of the
Constitution. He had already succeeded in competition for the design of the Philadelphia
Library. "When I traveled," he wrote, "I never
thought of architecture, but I got some books
and worked a few days, then gave a plan in the
ancient Ionic order, which carried the day. . . .
What will not Encouragement do? I afterward
had confidence enough to draw a Plan and
Elevations for the Capitol of the United States,
which after much deliberation, opposition, and
long Examinations, was adjudged to me."

Aided by a timely glimpse of Hallet's studies, he did indeed produce a design which, in spite of its minor incompetencies, received the prize. Its feature of appeal, which remained in the design of the old Capitol through all the vicissitudes of its building and rebuilding, was a low Roman dome.

The city of New York, already anticipating its future greatness, undertook its new City Hall, very ambitious for the day, which now stands amid towering skyscrapers as the milestone of a century of material growth. It was designed by Joseph Mangin, a Frenchman whose origin and fate are alike unknown, and built by John McComb. In its elements and style it is wholly French. The hollowed front with delicate columns one above another, against a rich arabesque of arched and grooved and paneled wall, the majestic circular staircase with its double flight, its dome above a ring of columns, are features familiar in many French buildings of the eighteenth century. Rarely had they been combined with more taste and a juster sense of proportion.

Among the colleges which now rapidly multi-

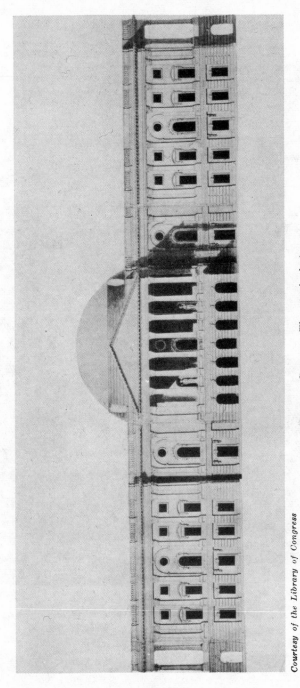

THE FEDERAL CAPITOL.—Thornton's design

Courtesy of Grosvenor Atterbury

FRANCE IN AMERICA
The New York City Hall

plied on every hand, the fruitful idea was again that of Jefferson. He wrote in 1810: "I consider the common plan followed in this country . . . of making one large and expensive building, as unfortunately erroneous. It is infinitely better to erect a small and separate lodge for each separate professorship, with only a hall below for his class, and two chambers above for himself; joining these lodges by barracks for a certain portion of the students, opening into a covered way, to give dry communication between all the schools. The whole of these arranged around an open square of grass and trees would make it, what it should be in fact, an academical village." This conception he realized in the University of Virginia, which remains to this day the most beautiful of American groups.

Up and down either side of the shaded Lawn are the tall, storied porticoes of the temple-like Pavilions, which once housed the classes of the ten schools as well as their heads. Between them, fronting the low dormitories, are the long white rows of the Colonnades. At the head, on the highest ground, stands the Rotunda, circular like the Roman Pantheon, with its dome and lofty spacious Corinthian porch. It is, in Jefferson's phrase, the perfect model of "spherical architecture," as the temples beside it are of the cubical. Beyond the lawn colonnades, facing outward, are second rows of dormitories, the Ranges with their red arches.

Ordered, calm, serene, it stirs our blood with a magic rarely felt on this side of the ocean. A single impress of form unites all the parts into an overwhelming artistic effect. The grandiose symmetry of disposition, the rhythmic alternation of pavilion and colonnade, the jewel-like simplicity of the major units, square-faceted and round, with their contrast like diamond and pearl, the eternal recurrence of the white columns, as a treble against the ground-bass of red walls, are elements of this effect which in its perfection surpasses analysis, and tells us we are in the presence of the supreme work of a great artist.

At Union College in Schenectady, Joseph Ramée, a French emigré, created at much the same time another ordered group of peaceful harmony of effect, and anticipated Jefferson by a few years in adopting, for the central unit, the monumental form of the Roman Pantheon.

FIRST WORKS UNDER REPUBLIC

With the growth of the towns under Hamilton's policy of favoring manufacture and commerce, types of buildings hitherto strange in America were called into being. The Bank of the United States in Philadelphia raised a proud marble front in imitation of the Exchange in Dublin. The first fine theaters were built to satisfy the taste created by wandering English companies, and nurtured by our travelers abroad. In New York the Park Theater, with its many balconies and pilastered front, was the work of the French royalist, Marc Isambard Brunel, during his brief sojourn. In Boston, where Puritan scruples were now relaxing, Bulfinch built a theater of monumental effect, richly adorned.

In the houses of leaders of society in the young republic there came, along with new ideas of form, the idea of modern convenience which had originated in the France of Louis XV. The old plan with central hall tended to give place to more flexible arrangements, with more numerous and distinct elements, and with greater privacy. The reception-rooms, living quarters, and service arrangements were segregated with a new care. Suites of bedrooms and dressing-rooms

[85]

were created, sometimes with alcove beds *à la français.* Service pantries made their appearance, stairways multiplied and were secluded from the stranger's gaze. In the finest town houses, like those of William Bingham in Philadelphia and Harrison Gray Otis on Beacon Street in Boston, the reception-rooms formed a suite in a principal story raised a story from the street.

A notable resource was gained by the use of forms of greater variety, to overcome the monotony of the rectangle in Colonial buildings. The octagon, the circle and the ellipse enriched the possibilities of composition in both mass and space, which were now studied with a new solicitude. The favorite plan among the members of the "Republican Court" was the French scheme with a projecting salon occupying the place of honor in the center of the garden front. Jefferson had already adopted this at Monticello, with an octagonal salon, before the Revolution. In its typical French form, almost universal under Louis XV, the salon was elliptical. Such an elliptical drawing-room, placed to one side, first appears here in William Hamilton's great

Photograph by A. J. Weed

ROME IN AMERICA
The University of Virginia

AN ADAM INTERIOR

The oval drawing room at Lemon Hill, Philadelphia

house, the Woodlands, at Philadelphia. It is a house remarkable for its freedom and novelty of composition, both as regards convenience and privacy, and as regards variety of spatial effects achieved by its circular columned vestibule, its curving stairs, its great semicircular bays and niches. The elliptical salon in the center figured in Hoban's winning design for the President's House—the White House—in the houses of Alexander Hamilton, Secretary of the Treasury, of General Knox, Secretary of War, and of such leaders of wealth and fashion as Joseph Barrell, Theodore Lyman, Governor Gore and Harrison Gray Otis about Boston, Henry Pratt in Philadelphia, and Nathaniel Russell in Charleston. Many of these in New England were from the designs of Bulfinch, as were those built with circular salons, more in harmony with classical taste, for James Swan and Jonathan Mason.

Classical influence showed itself, otherwise than in the plan, in two quite different ways. One was the use of the delicate Adam proportions and details, suggested by the ornaments newly become familiar in the excavation of the buried cities. The other involved the adoption

of the monumental portico and heavy proportions of the temple. One dominated the North;
the other, the South.

The first employment of the Adam forms was
in the ceilings of plaster in slight relief, so characteristic of the style. Washington himself led the
way in work executed at Mount Vernon during
the darkest days of the war. When John Penn
came to America, the year after the peace, to
build on the banks of the Schuylkill his little
country seat, Solitude, the rich Adam ceilings of
urns and garlands, of rosettes and candelabra, of
airy scrolls and chimeras, were almost its sole
ornaments. At the Woodlands, soon after, the
doorways, too, had the new classical enrichments,
and the entrance front showed slender Adam
proportions, while the portico toward the river
was of contrasting monumental grandeur. Two
vanished houses in Philadelphia, Bingham's great
town house, modeled on Manchester house in
London, and the vast mansion built for the President, helped to establish the style. The impulse
to further imitation of the older Louis XV style,
which might have been given by the marble
"folly" begun by L'Enfant for Robert Morris,

was lost when Morris became bankrupt and the unfinished house was demolished.

In New England, Bulfinch introduced the new manner with tall pilasters of slight projection, light cornices and balustrades, shallow surface arches, slender colonnettes, narrow window-bars, fanlights and side-lights with tenuous tracery of metal, mantels with delicate imported composition ornaments of festoons, urns and classical figures. His Boston houses in Beacon Street, Park Street, Tremont Street and in the vanished Franklin Crescent, first of the coherent blocks of city residences, gave the models. In Salem his faithful pupil, Samuel McIntire, the gifted carver, executed the fabulous and ill-fated Derby mansion—thought "more like a palace than the dwelling of an American merchant"—on lines Bulfinch suggested, and gave the town its present impress. To Portland the new doctrine was brought by Alexander Parris; to New Haven, by David Hoadley; to western Massachusetts, by Asher Benjamin, who made Bulfinch's formulæ universally available by his publications. In New York and Albany, McComb and Philip Hooker shared the same tendencies.

AMERICAN ARCHITECTURE

On the borders of Chesapeake Bay, Thornton gave admirable models of the Adam style in Homewood, near Baltimore, in the Octagon at Washington, in Tudor Place at Georgetown. Even in Virginia, the stronghold of the monumental classic, the delicate Adam treatment made the effect of the lovely Barton Myers house in Norfolk. At Charleston the chimney-pieces showed the same decorative motives as those of distant Salem and Portland.

The builders did not always use ornaments cast from London molds. Robert Wellford, who claimed to be the first American maker of composition ornament, not only imitated these, but put on the market patriotic subjects such as the Battle of Lake Erie and the eagle mourning over the tomb of departed heroes. Local house-joiners even developed their own means of suggesting the Adam effects by simple use of their ordinary tools. Rosettes and garlands were made with flutings and nicks of the gouge, or with auger holes of varied sizes. These ingenious adaptations to tool and material are among the most charming of minor American architectural devices.

Courtesy of Arthur Lyman

AN ADAM HOUSE IN NEW ENGLAND

The Lyman House at Waltham, Massachusetts

Photograph by Roger Millen

A HOUSE OF THE PIEDMONT

Monticello, the home of Jefferson

FIRST WORKS UNDER REPUBLIC

Meanwhile, however, the example of Jefferson was giving a direct impulse to more rigorous and severe classical treatment in house building. Retired from Washington's administration, he undertook the remodeling of Monticello in a more Roman style. The attics were pulled down to give an effect of a single story as in Roman houses and their French adaptations; a Roman dome was added over the salon as in the Hôtel de Salm. In the great houses of his friends in the Piedmont, at Montpelier, Edgehill, Farmington, Ampthill, Barboursville and Bremo, he used the massive square white portico with telling effect against the walls of brick. When he became President he ordained for the White House the great circular portico of the river front, the long colonnades of the offices at either side. In the University of Virginia, at the end of his career, he finally achieved his prophetic early ambition to fit the whole house within the rectangular mass of the temple, an extreme of classical ardor which had no parallel abroad. The students spread his example all up and down the South.

VIII

THE GREEK REVIVAL

CHAPTER VIII

THE GREEK REVIVAL

HARD on the heels of the first adoption of Roman forms came the Greek. The leader here was a newcomer, Benjamin Henry Latrobe, a professional of thorough training who had learned his Greek details in England. He found himself in an atmosphere of classical enthusiasm greater than that of England itself—of allusions from Plutarch to Brutus and to Cincinnatus, with whom the Revolutionary patriots had been identified. He supplied the knowledge, but the stimulus to bodily imitation of ancient buildings came from the initiative of Jefferson and the fervor of clients and laymen.

Latrobe's opportunity came at the turn of the century, with the building of the Bank of Pennsylvania—destroyed, alas, long ago. It was all of marble. The general form was rectangular, with porticoes at each front of six graceful Ionic columns, their capitals modeled on those of the

Erechtheum. In the center was the circular banking-hall, domed in masonry on the pattern of the Pantheon. Beaujour, the French major, "a man of great talents . . . long in Greece and Egypt . . . a perfect judge of the fine arts," summed up its qualities in the phrase, *"Si beau, et si simple."*

On the exterior, at the side, there are many little departures from the antique model which show that the architect was not altogether happy in the straight-jacket of the temple form. Latrobe himself testified, after the death of the bank's president, Samuel M. Fox, that the "existence and taste" of the building were due to him. Thornton, Latrobe's great antagonist, likewise bore witness to this by putting satirically this remark into his mouth: "The Bank of Pennsylvania I know has been much admired, but it would have been much handsomer if Joseph Fox and the late John Blakely, Esqrs. directors, had not confined me to a copy of the Parthenon at Athens." Thus the authorities of the bank, who owed much to Latrobe's skill, appear to have been ultimately responsible for the essentially American literalness of its classicism.

THE BEGINNINGS OF THE GREEK REVIVAL.—The Bank of Pennsylvania, Latrobe's design

THE TRIUMPH OF THE GREEK REVIVAL

The Bank of the United States, Philadelphia

THE GREEK REVIVAL

Jefferson, who had become President in 1801, was quick to see Latrobe's ability and to give him official encouragement as he had the other men of high training. He created the post of Surveyor of the Public Buildings of the United States and placed Latrobe in charge both at the Capitol and at the White House. The old Hall of Representatives, burned by the British, was a triumph of their collaboration. The House and Senate Chambers as Latrobe rebuilt them after the War of 1812 were Greek hemicycles of great dignity. By his personal stamina, and by the support of Jefferson, Latrobe was able to survive the onslaughts of Thornton, by which his predecessors, Hallet and Hadfield, had been borne under, and to establish the first professional office of an architect in the United States, with a wide practise. His pupils Robert Mills and William Strickland carried on his tradition, which dominated American architecture to the middle of the nineteenth century.

Already by its second decade Greek enthusiasm was at a high pitch. Nicholas Biddle, who in his precocious youth had selected the casts from the Musée Napoleon for the Pennsylvania

Academy of the Fine Arts, and had undertaken the journey to Greece, was the arbiter of taste. For his magazine, the *Port-Folio,* George Tucker, one of Jefferson's protégés, wrote urging a veritable revival of Greek architecture.

When the second Bank of the United States undertook its new banking house in Philadelphia the advertisement for plans stated that "the Directors are desirous of exhibiting a chaste imitation of Grecian architecture, in its simplest form." Latrobe, in his design, took the final step of reproducing the Parthenon, with two fronts of eight Greek Doric columns. Strickland and others also gave Greek designs, and it was to Strickland that the execution, closely following Latrobe's plans, ultimately fell after his master's departure and death.

In the day of its building the Bank attracted an attention which was international. Bernhard of Saxe-Weimar wrote in 1825: "It is the most beautiful building I have yet seen in the United States." The highest praise is that of a correspondent of the *London Morning Chronicle,* in the 'thirties, who writes that the building "excells in elegance and equals in utility, the edifice, not only of the Bank of England, but of any banking house in the world."

These estimates were dependent on the universal success of the Greek revival, which elsewhere ultimately reached the same goal. In Great Britain the form of the Parthenon had been adopted for the National Monument at Edinburgh. In Germany it had been embodied in the Walhalla at Regensburg. These, however, were monuments simply. It scarcely occurred to architects abroad to follow the great Athenian model in a building devoted to practical uses. The Bank of the United States not only anticipates the foreign versions of the Parthenon by a decade but represents an extreme of classicism unparalleled abroad. The form of the temple was established as a single unconditional ideal for all classes of buildings.

For the Connecticut capitol at New Haven, Ithiel Town built a model of the Theseum; for the Kentucky capitol at Frankfort it was an Ionic temple which was preferred. New York, too, had to have its Parthenon, the old Custom House, now the Sub-Treasury, built by Town and Alexander Jackson Davis. The banks of

Wall Street of the 'thirties might well suggest the row of treasuries at Olympia. For Girard College in Philadelphia, Biddle overrode the opposition of the architect, Thomas U. Walter, to force the adoption of the temple form executed with a vast Greek Corinthian order.

Where the full scheme of the temple was not adopted at least there was a great colonnade, as in Mills' façade of the Treasury in Washington, Town's, in the Merchants' Exchange in New York, and in Walter's wings of the national Capitol. Strickland carried a circular peristyle about the front of the Exchange in Philadelphia, and placed the Monument of Lysicrates, as a convenient cupola, on top.

The commemorative monuments also took their forms from antiquity. In the competition for the Washington Monument in Baltimore, Ramée proposed a triumphal arch, Mills, a vast Greek column. Greece and the column carried off the palm. The design of the monument, powerful and utterly simple, anticipates those of the Wellington monuments in London and Dublin, and has set the example for many others. For the monument at Bunker Hill an obelisk

Photograph by James F. Hughes

THE GREEK COLUMN

The Washington Monument in Baltimore

Photograph by Philip B. Wallace

THE GREEK HOUSE
Andalusia on the Delaware

was preferred, and this was the type with which Mills won the competition for the Washington Monument in the national capital, completed only after the Civil War. In its day it was the tallest of man-made structures. Before its completion all extraneous appendages had been eliminated. The character of classic architecture and the character of Washington are well matched in its noble simplicity and quiet grandeur.

The first church to show the classic inspiration was Latrobe's Catholic Cathedral in Baltimore for the diocese of the United States, begun after the opening of the century. Here a Roman scheme was adopted, with simple granite walls, a low masonry dome over the crossing, a great portico at the west. The interior had a new richness in composition of interior space, a new majesty. Even to-day, a century after its building, the Cathedral remains the finest classical church in the country.

For Saint John's, the Episcopal church in Washington, Latrobe chose the scheme of the Greek cross with equal arms, now disguised by later additions. To his pupil Mills, fell the task of adapting the classic forms to the requirements of the newer evangelical sects. For the auditorium which their emphasis on the sermon required he used a great domed rotunda, circular or octagonal. Of all his churches of this type there remains only the Monumental Church in Richmond, in which he used the Egyptian details first popularized by Napoleon's eastern campaign.

Considerations of use were ultimately thrust aside in the church, also, by visions of the temple. Jefferson built one, Roman in suggestion, for Christ Church in Charlottesville. For the French chapel in New York, Davis followed the Ionic temple on the Illissus. In St. Paul's Church in Boston and in many others the simple severity of the temple was also preferred, the Christian purpose revealed only by the Cross.

The dwelling was the last to yield to the ruling Greek mania, but yield it did, and the triumph of the classic was universal. Critics who have felt that the passing of the Colonial marked the end of healthy development of traditional art as an outgrowth of contemporary culture, and that the classic revival was an exotic with no firm root in American civilization forget that the men of the 'twenties and 'thirties had a consciousness of solidarity with ancient Greece which reached every department of life. Their enthusiasm was fanned into flame by the Greek war of independence. There was even the demand for military intervention. A Congressman from western New York declared he could furnish, from his sparsely settled region, "five hundred men, six feet high, with sinewy arms and case-hardened constitutions, bold spirits and daring adventurers, who would march on a bushel of corn and a gallon of whisky per man from the extreme part of the world to Constantinople."

Jefferson's Roman temples for his professors, realizing his dream of a generation before, had been the first of the temple houses. Hadfield translated one into Greek at Arlington, the home of Washington's adopted son, whose daughter was later to bring it to her husband, the commander of the Confederate armies, Robert E. Lee. Hadfield used a front of six Doric columns of enormous massiveness, following those of the great temple at Pæstum. Disproportionate as it seems from near at hand, no other house than Arlington could carry so well across the

Potomac, no other so well hold its own at the other end of a composition with the Capitol.

The extreme step in the imitation of the temple, the placing of columns all about instead of merely in front, was taken by Biddle in enlarging his house, Andalusia, on the Delaware in 1834. He followed the Theseum at Athens which he had seen and admired in his youth. It remained only to model a house on the Parthenon, with its front of eight columns instead of six. This was done by James Coles Bruce at his Virginia plantation, Berry Hill. Bruce had stayed in Philadelphia just before inheriting the estate, and was influenced by Andalusia in his choice of a type. On either side of its great lawn are the office and schoolhouse, each likewise in the form of a Greek Doric temple. Nowhere else, perhaps, is the ante-bellum plantation to be found in equal magnificence.

South and North, East and West, such examples were followed in houses large and small. Whenever towns and regions prospered in the 'thirties and 'forties, the white porticoes were to be found, fronting or surrounding the houses. In the academic shades of Cambridge, of Athens in Georgia—significant by its very name—in the whaling ports of Nantucket and New Bedford, in the blue grass of Kentucky, they flourished alike. In New York, Colonnade Row on Lafayette Street sheltered Fenimore Cooper, Philip Hone, and Washington Irving. Along the Gulf it was particularly common to have the columns surrounding the house, with balconies between, suitable to the climate.

In the backwoods states beyond the Alleghenies and the Ohio the imitation of the temple was even more universal than on the seaboard. When the wave of Eastern emigration of the 'thirties swept out along the newly opened Erie Canal and across the lakes it brought with it the classic ideal. The names of towns—Rome and Syracuse and Troy in western New York; Ypsilanti and Byron, Ionia and Scio in Michigan—recall classic sites, or personalities and places in the Greek struggle for freedom. Many a little old township in the Northwest has no house which does not conform to the ruling taste, yet such were the possible variations that no two are alike. Square piers might be substituted for the round columns, Greek moldings suggested with astonishing success by the simplifications of the carpenter.

With forms so thoroughly established, owners were able to proceed with no other assistance than that of the builders. The few professional architects of the time, mostly in the eastern centers, generally refused to abdicate their creative liberty to the temple scheme in dwelling-houses, so that it represents a genuinely popular preference of laymen and amateurs.

Along with the rectangular temple, the passion for unity of form brought the centralized scheme,—square, octagonal or circular,—descendant of the *villa rotonda*. Latrobe employed this for his Center House of the Philadelphia Water Works, a dome sheltering the tank. Jefferson, who had three times proposed Palladio's model for others without success, finally built for his own retreat at Poplar Forest a house which was a perfect octagon. Years later Orson Squire Fowler built another on the Hudson, and by his publications spread the idea widely. In the 'fifties octagonal houses were scattered everywhere. Even the ultimate step of building the house in the form of a circle—long imagined by enthusiasts—was finally taken. The victory of the formal ideal was complete.

Jefferson's dream thus came true—to establish the classic as a national style. While it had triumphed in every country, in the older nations of Europe, with firmly established traditions, its success had been tempered by conservatism and common sense. Only on the outskirts of European civilization, in Scotland, in Russia, in America was enthusiasm sophomoric enough to carry through the full classic program. Only in America was it pushed to its extreme consequences. The attempt can not be judged merely from our present standpoint. In 1800 it was not banal, but original, to copy the Greeks. Whatever we think of the work of the revivalists, we must recognize that they endowed America with an architectural tradition unsurpassed in dignity and monumental quality. Whether we like it or not we must recognize it as one of the distinctive American contributions to style. It furnished the basis for the ingrained love of the simple, austere, refined and chastened in architecture which underlies the spirit of our creative work to-day.

IX

ROMANTICISM AND THE GOTHIC

CHAPTER IX

ROMANTICISM AND THE GOTHIC

LIKE all artistic creations, the classic edifice, in the moment of its highest splendor, was being undermined by the work of a new generation. The classicists were followed by the romantics.

Although romanticism with its glorification of the individual was rooted in the very essence of American democracy, the first stimulus came from abroad, especially from England, where the romantic movement had long been gathering strength. The modern appreciation of landscape had begun early in the eighteenth century. Kent "leaped the fence and saw that all nature was a garden." England and Germany awakened to their northern national heritage: the mythology and legend, the history and art of the Middle Ages. Walpole wrote his *Castle of Otranto* and built his Gothic villa, Strawberry Hill. Although the full fruits of the seed were not garnered until after 1800, with the genera-

[111]

tion of Byron and Scott and Hugo, of Constable
and Delacroix, there began already an increasing
harvest. To the romantic enthusiasts, pictur-
esqueness and naturalness, nationality and religion, all seemed embodied not in classic architecture, but in the Gothic.

Even in America where classic influence was
so strong there was soon a romantic undercurrent. Jefferson, whose choice of a mountaintop
as the site for his classic house was itself a
romantic act, brought in the English landscape
garden. Side by side with the first calm Greek
monuments rose others, few at first, which took
their inspiration from the Middle Ages.

Even before the Revolution Jefferson had proposed a Gothic garden temple. Latrobe gave
the cathedral builders in Baltimore an alterna-
tive Gothic design, in which he came quite
abreast of the best English knowledge of the
style at that time. In a Philadelphia country-
seat, Sedgeley, he made, just before the eighteenth century closed, the first American attempt to revive the Gothic mansion. Its little
lodge still stands, though modified out of recognition. Godefroi, a French refugee in Balti-

more, built for the Sulpicians the Chapel of St. Mary, with Gothic forms but poorly understood. It was the first church of the Gothic revival in America.

Latrobe, Mills and Strickland all indulged in Gothic exercises as an occasional relief from the classic. Latrobe's Bank of Philadelphia, vaulted throughout in masonry, was the earliest and worthiest of these buildings. It has long been swept away, as have the first gimcrack churches and Masonic temples of Strickland and his contemporaries in Philadelphia and New York. As time went on others gained a firmer grasp of the style and established it in the far South at Charleston and at Savannah. At Milledgeville, the old capital of Georgia, the state buildings were made Gothic in the 'thirties. Alexander Jackson Davis, another devotee of the classic for public buildings, likewise took up Gothic forms. He used them for the old New York University building on Washington Square, and built a great Gothic country-seat for Robert Gilmor of Baltimore, a pioneer collector of old masters. Washington Irving, in remodeling Sunnyside, his house at Tarrytown, gave the romantic movement a new impetus. Robert Dale Owen, before building the Smithsonian Institution in Washington, reached the conclusion, by an elaborate train of reasoning, that the Romanesque phase of medieval art was best suited to be a national style. The structure, erected from the designs of James Renwick, had a picturesque grouping of towers.

On the seaboard by the end of the 'thirties people began to tire of the endless repetition of the temple house. Rational and satiric literary onslaughts against it were made by Cooper and others. The "English cottage style" was championed by Andrew Jackson Downing, the first American to make a profession of landscape gardening. Davis joined with him in publishing books which gave numerous models. The cottages of wood and stucco, with steep roofs, traceried eaves and latticed windows, multiplied rapidly in the North, while in the South some of the finest plantation houses were now Gothic. Davis built Belmead, above Richmond, on the lines of a famous English house, East Barsham. Staunton Hill, one of the two great Bruce plantations, opposed its Gothic gables and porches to the Greek porticoes of the other, Berry Hill.

Meanwhile in England, Pugin was beginning to preach a revival of "Christian architecture" with a new fervor, and to practise it with a new knowledge. At least for churches, the Gothic forms were now felt to be more appropriate. Trinity Church in New York, which had never abandoned the old tradition of Gothic, entrusted its architectural fortunes in 1839 to Richard Upjohn, a newcomer from England. He built the church still standing at the head of Wall Street, in honest materials, with competent familiarity with the rich forms of English Gothic. Renwick likewise displayed an accomplished mastery of Gothic structure and dispositions in Grace Church and St. Patrick's Cathedral in New York.

More solid and more simple than these churches were buildings of another class for which the military architecture of the Middle Ages suggested a Gothic form. These were the prisons, to which the reformers of the 'thirties gave great attention. The improvement of the horrible conditions prevailing in prisons of an earlier day had been one of the first cares of the founders of the Republic. Jefferson had sent to Virginia from Paris a plan for a prison on the principle of solitary confinement, which was adopted a decade later by Latrobe in the Penitentiary at Richmond. At the same time Mangin designed a prison for New York, with workshops as well as cells. The scheme with cell-blocks radiating from a central rotunda, which ultimately became universal, was evolved a generation later by John Haviland of Philadelphia. The governments of France, England, Prussia and Russia sent commissions to study the American prison system and obtain designs from him. An architect of merit, he gave even to his prisons an impress of artistic form. The vast stone front of the Eastern Penitentiary in Philadelphia has still to be surpassed by the American worshipers of medieval forms.

X

A CONFUSION OF TONGUES

CHAPTER X

A CONFUSION OF TONGUES

THE choice between classic and Gothic, which Latrobe first offered to the Cathedral trustees, rapidly widened to include other styles. The struggle between them did not issue, as it had in earlier centuries, with the victory of either one, but both continued, subdivided further, and received the addition of many more. The reason, here as abroad, lay in the growth of historical knowledge, one of the most characteristic products of the nineteenth century, which for the first time made the forms of many styles familiar to a single generation. The historical spirit had already contributed largely to the growth of classicism and romanticism, and to their division into Roman and Greek, Gothic and Romanesque phases. To these were now added styles unconnected with the classic and romantic programs. Soon there was created among designers the conscious principle of complete freedom of

[119]

choice between the various historical styles. A given style was adopted on grounds of personal preference or supposed suitability to the problem in hand. The "Battle of the Styles" was on.

At first the field of choice was wide, and the contestants were informed with little knowledge of many of the styles they championed. Even the "Italian villas" would scarcely have been recognized in Italy. The "chalets" and "Moorish cottages," however, and such phantasms as Barnum's house, Iranistan, at Bridgeport, were, after all, exceptions. More pervasive was the French influence of the Second Empire. The French architect Lemoulnier brought the style to Boston in the middle of the century. Made popular by the completion of the Louvre and the Hôtel de Ville, it was taken up officially, horribly brutalized, in a multitude of government offices and public buildings after the Civil War, such as the State Department in Washington, the old Post Offices of New York, Philadelphia, and Boston. In dwellings the mansard roof covered the land.

Less serious than the mere variety of style, which here, as in Europe, left the craftsman unsustained by solid traditions of form, was the vulgarization of all styles in the bourgeois democracy of the growing towns. Never in the world had means been more diffused than in the North after the Civil War. Never had there been so raw a society as that which sprang up in the newer western regions. The democracy of Old Hickory and of the first settlement of the Northwest had at least acknowledged the gods of the classic Olympus. In the crude towns of the gold rush and of the boomers the only guides were whim and ostentation. The parvenus of the East had none better. The American individualism which demanded a house different from that of one's neighbor was unrestrained by the taste of a settled aristocracy, the tenacity of peasants, or the impotence of a herded proletariat.

What have been called the "Dark Ages" of American architecture have indeed often been painted blacker than they were. There was no time when good work was not being done. The last of the old leaders and traditions survived to overlap with the new. Each of the passing movements produced certain works which have merit and value. What was unique in degree perhaps, as compared with Europe at the same time or with America before or since, was the relative submergence of these leaders and these works in the mass of vulgarity. The leaders were still few, the mass, greater than ever before, still unleavened.

The machine was then a new toy, every fresh triumph of which was eagerly acclaimed. The power scroll-saw was quickly seized on as offering a substitute for tracery and carving. Its fantastic brackets supported the wide eaves of the Victorian house, its curves filled the panels. The casting of iron made the duplication of molded detail easy. At first used frankly in light balconies and railings, it was later sanded and painted in imitation of stone, for the multiplication of the orders over the fronts of warehouses and shops, and even for the great dome added to the enlarged Capitol in Washington. In brickmaking and bricklaying mechanical perfection of shape, uniformity of color, smoothness of surface and fineness of jointing became the ruling ideas. The technical ability to make glass in large sheets was turned to account in houses as well as in shops, with an avidity which did not discriminate between public display and domestic intimacy.

The prevailing confusion was increased by the vast new influx of immigrants from Europe. They flocked into the lands opened by the Pacific railways, and to the factories flourishing behind tariff barriers and eager for foreign labor not yet accustomed to the American standard of means and comfort. Among the Germans who fled from the repressions of 'forty-eight or the aggressive Prussian policy of the 'sixties were many men of technical capacity, to whom fell much of the work of the decade following the Civil War. In Germany itself, however, taste was then at an ebb. The forms of the florid northern Renaissance which these men imported, and which burgeoned in the street architecture of the 'seventies, added to the rank disorder.

In the midst of a like wilderness in Victorian England, the voice of Ruskin was raised in praise of an other-worldliness which would restore sacrifice to religion, truth to construction. Recoiling from the materialism and industrialism of the time, he could see salvation only in a pious return to the spirit of the Middle Ages, which he found embodied only in its own forms. Thus the Gothic received a new impetus. His identification of artistic merit with moral qualities— "truth" of structure, nobility of material, and human devotion as expressed in lavish adornment by carving and color, led his admiration to the southern, Italian work, and this became the chief ingredient of the later Victorian Gothic. American adherents were many. The churches were not the only buildings to feel their hands, which were exercised even on the very temples of materialism—the banks. Such institutions of taste as the Pennsylvania Academy of the Fine Arts, the National Academy of Design in New York, and the newly founded Boston Museum of Fine Arts all housed themselves, in the 'seventies, in palaces of a doubtful Gothic, supposedly Italian, with pointed arches of vari-colored stones. Memorial Hall at Harvard remains as the most ambitious and important monument of the style.

There were not lacking men who dared to laugh at "consistency of style" and to combine elements from many styles to create a hybrid, personal means of expression. Frank Furness of Philadelphia—in spite of his Academy—was one of these, whose buildings, now thought of more as aberrations, had the power to fire the youthful enthusiasm of a later apostle of individuality, Louis Sullivan.

Into the welter of prejudice, ignorance and wilfulness came a new generation of architects trained abroad in the great Paris school, the École des Beaux-Arts, which the empire of Napoleon III had given a fresh prestige. The first to make his influence felt was Henry Hobson Richardson, a Southerner, whom the outcome of the war sent north to the rarefied Boston of Emerson and Ruskin. Personally of enormous vigor, Richardson was not at home in the fashionable Victorian Gothic of his first essays. In Trinity Church he turned to the cruder and more elemental Romanesque of southern France and Spain, in which, as he went on, he discerned a suitability to American conditions and environment. Towers and broad low arches in picturesque array were mantled with the rugged stonework of Auvergne. Painters, carvers and craftsmen, enlisted with a new enthusiasm, worked side by side in the decoration. In town halls and jails, libraries and college buildings of the 'eighties, Richardson applied and varied his bold formulæ. He was followed by a host of imitators, who caught his mannerisms without his spirit. Few had the forebearance to build simply, without picturesque adjuncts, as he did on occasion, as in the vast, ordered and severe warehouse for Marshall Field. Foreign observers saw in his rustic lodges of great boulders an image of what they thought architecture in a new continent ought to be.

Richard Morris Hunt had preceded Richardson to the Beaux-Arts. On his first return to America before the war he had established an atelier in which some of the leaders of the next generation were trained. He had, however, soon gone back to France, and it was after 1870 when he came again to America and began to give to the plutocratic society of New York and Newport the setting it awaited. The descendants of the first capitalists, like the Vanderbilts and Astors, were adopting a life of material splendor patterned on that of the older European aristocracies. Hunt, forceful and unintimidated by his clients, established the style of their town and

Courtesy of the Pennsylvania Museum

THE EARLY GOTHIC REVIVAL

The Eastern Penitentiary, Philadelphia

Courtesy of the Architectural Record

GILDED REMINISCENCES—Biltmore

country palaces, drawing his suggestions from the châteaux of the Valois. The great mansions of Fifth Avenue took their type from his houses for William K. Vanderbilt, for John Jacob Astor, for Commodore Gerry; the Newport "cottages," from his "Ochre Court," "The Breakers," and "Marble House."

The finest, perhaps, was the first-named, already within two generations a prey of the wrecker, like most of the other great town houses of that era. Still romantic, high roofed, turreted, and many chimneyed, it offered its rich façades and vast monumental rooms as a background for the exotic pageantry of America's first gilded age.

More splendid still was Biltmore, the Vanderbilt château in North Carolina, where Hunt strove to create for his clients an illusion truly feudal. Blois itself was pillaged for the idea of the great staircase. Accomplished detail and fine masonry made the *pastiche* no unworthy one. For the decoration Hunt gathered around him a group of artists who worked with an enthusiasm of emulation in what they felt to be a true artistic Renaissance.

Meanwhile, in the minor house architecture, a

new force was making itself felt—the English "Queen Anne." William Morris, the father of the revival of handicraft in the Arts and Crafts movement, in his "Red House" on Bexley Heath had started a return to the homely domestic building of brick in the days of Anne, when medieval and classic motives were still freely mingled. Half-timber, clustered chimneys, rough-cast gables, barred casements, and molded sheathing—favorite motives with English designers of the school, like Norman Shaw—appeared in America with the English building at the Centennial Exposition. At first they were borrowed with little thought, as in the houses by a host of imitators of Shaw and Eastlake, or the fashionable casinos at Newport and Short Hills by the new firm of McKim, Mead and White.

These men, however, had grasped the deeper implications of the movement, which involved not the copying of current English idioms but the study of local characteristics and materials in the early American vernacular. The three men, even before they formed their partnership, took, in company with Bigelow, what they came afterward to call their "famous trip" along the

New England coast, in the Centennial year.
They saw the old houses of Salem and Portsmouth, the fragments assembled at Indian Hill
by the pioneer collector, Ben Perley Poore. On
their return they launched a Colonial revival,
which, fantastic at first in its mixture and overloading of detail, gradually gained adherents,
knowledge and strength. The old materials, the
"Harvard brick" of New England, the ledgestone of Pennsylvania were taken up and given
once more a sympathetic handling.

In Florida, John Carrère and Thomas Hastings, just back from their training abroad,
inaugurated a return to the local Spanish traditions in their great hotels, their church and
houses there.

In Philadelphia two young men, Walter Cope
and John Stewardson, early cut off by death,
adopted English collegiate models—Tudor or
Elizabethan—at Bryn Mawr, at Princeton, at
Pennsylvania and elsewhere. Their loving study
of simple textures was to be perpetuated with
richer forms by a whole school—Eyre and Day
and Klauder and their successors—and was
ultimately, with the complete adoption of the

style by Princeton and Yale, to have a wide influence in American universities, as well as in domestic building.

The romantic strain, so strong in Richardson, lived on in the Gothic of Bertram Goodhue and of his erstwhile partner Ralph Adams Cram. The early Gothic revivalists, as well as the first followers of Ruskin, had mastered the forms rather than the spirit of the Middle Ages. Meanwhile Morris had taught his lesson, Sedding and Bodley in England had worked more freely in their chosen style, with greater sympathy for materials and craftsmanship. These qualities now appeared in the American Gothic.

Cram was a fervent literary disciple of Ruskin, Morris and the leaders of the Oxford movement; Goodhue was a winsome youth who had read Goethe almost in the nursery and at fifteen had blazoned on his wall the motto: "Art pre-exists in Nature, and Nature is reproduced in Art." He had absorbed Gothic forms in Renwick's office. They flowed magically from his gifted pen which created marvelous dream cities of Germany, of medieval Italy, of Persia. Together the young knights-errant went forth lance in hand, to tilt against the powers of industrialism, to rescue piety and craftsmanship.

Their first success was won in alliance with the High Churchmen. They took up the ritual arrangements and the traditional forms of the English church as they had been cut off by Henry VIII. All Saints' at Ashmont, their earliest triumph, built in 1892, shows a free use of this last phase of Gothic, with walls of brown-seamed granite, and windows of rich glass, heavily leaded. In their later churches they were to range more widely within the styles of the Middle Ages, from the Early English of Cram's Calvary Church in Pittsburgh to the Byzantine of Goodhue's St. Bartholomew in New York. At West Point the craggy site of the Military Academy suggested a castellated treatment with a superbly rugged chapel. Although for years Goodhue shunned Italy for fear of exposing himself to the spell of the classic, he did not disdain to work occasionally with classic forms, and achieved notable success with them in his California houses. In Cuba and California, too, he was to work in the lavish Spanish Colonial style with fine imaginative effect.

[131]

AMERICAN ARCHITECTURE

As time went on Goodhue's Gothic was to become less and less a matter of archæology. The English work of Sir Gilbert Scott turned him in a freer direction. St. Vincent Ferrer in New York already shows the influence of Scott's Liverpool Cathedral. After Goodhue's first sight of Liverpool, he redesigned completely his proposed cathedral in Baltimore, with bolder scale and less traditional details. This was but the first step in a development which was to carry him away from historical forms, into a struggle for freedom of expression, the story of which belongs to a later chapter.

XI

THE STAGE OF MODERNISM:
NEW MATERIALS AND NEW TYPES

CHAPTER XI

THE STAGE OF MODERNISM: NEW MATERIALS AND NEW TYPES

UNTIL late in the nineteenth century architects had worked primarily with the traditional materials, wood, stone and brick, and at the conventional problems of the house, the church, the college, the civic building, at most the theater and the bank. Meanwhile modern industrial civilization was coming both to furnish them with new materials of revolutionary properties, and to present them with problems in the creation of new types of buildings for industry, transportation and commerce. Iron and steel, concrete reinforced with steel, were of a strength hitherto unknown in building. The stations and bridges called into being by the railways, the vast factories which ease of communication encouraged, the offices for business thus built up have little precedent in earlier epochs and are the characteristic structures of our time.

[135]

AMERICAN ARCHITECTURE

The industrial revolution, with its division of labor and application of power machinery, had begun in England in the later eighteenth century, and had soon adopted the steam engine, its first great servant. Dependence on English goods had led Hamilton, as one of the first cares of the new state, to encourage American manufactures. L'Enfant laid out for him a grandiose plan for the new industrial town of Paterson at the falls of the Passaic; Latrobe designed for the Philadelphia Water Works the first steam engine in America. Fulton with his steamboat solved the problem of communication by water on the great rivers and lakes, as well as ultimately on the ocean. The steam railroad, invented in England, found its chief use in the vast areas of the United States. In the wake of industrialism came the capitalistic organization of society, with its great cities, its vast accumulations of wealth, its laboring masses, its imperialistic exploitation of backward regions.

Although factory towns using the power of the rivers had appeared in New England soon after 1800, the country remained overwhelmingly agricultural until the Civil War. Transportation and commerce dealt more with the export of raw materials and agricultural products, the import of finer manufactured goods. The stimulus to manufacture given by the war was perpetuated by the high tariff imposed to pay the debt and to insure the rich American market to American factories. The vast unoccupied lands invited the monopolizing of natural resources; the absence of legal restraints on internal trade promoted combinations on a grand scale. New technical inventions—the typewriter, the sewing machine—stimulated by the scarcity and cost of labor, were exploited at home and abroad.

The natural wealth of open land and the democracy which it had evoked kept the prosperity of the many on a high level. The "American System" came into being. It involved not so much the grinding down of the masses to produce goods cheaply for sale abroad, as the development of their own capacity to buy more and more material luxuries. The demand was created by democratic passion for equality of standards and by the vast development of advertising among a population enabled to read by universal free education. Thus quantity production could be developed on an unexampled scale, in the midst of a bourgeois prosperity never before approached. The consequences were felt not least in building, which has become one of the greatest of industries in the United States.

Of the new materials, iron was the first to find extensive application, in trusses over assembly halls and concourses of unprecedented width, and bridges of wide span. Cast into columns, iron permitted a new slenderness of interior supports.

The international expositions, beginning with the Crystal Palace in London in 1851, had given a great stimulus to the use of large areas of glass, which the development of plate glass arose to satisfy. The shops, the vast department-stores, became so many show-cases of which the walls tended to disappear, the exterior points of support to be as few and far apart as possible. The skylight, on the other hand, enabled museums and exhibition buildings to be made without openings in their walls, with great courts roofed with glass and iron. These new possibilities, like all new resources, were exploited at first without appreciation of their corresponding drawbacks.

With the development of new processes, steel succeeded wrought and cast iron in construction. Rolled into beams of form mathematically devised to give the greatest resistance to bending, it permitted level floor spans to have greater width than ever before. In the 'eighties such rolled beams were imported and still precious. In channels, angles and plates steel could be riveted together in a rigid frame of unprecedented strength.

At first the supposition was that metal, being noncombustible, was proof against fire, but steel was soon found to twist and bend in fire with disastrous results. It proved necessary to case the metal in fireproofing, preferably brick or terra cotta which had been through fire in its very making. The impulse to the arts of fire and clay was great. Not only structural terra cotta, but glazed faience of white and of the greatest variety of colors became available. Pressed in molds, it permitted a multiplication of ornament that was to be far from an unmixed blessing.

Latest of the new materials to receive wide

application was concrete. The Romans, with their remarkable volcanic cement, had developed a system of massive concrete construction well adapted to their imperial requirements and their vast bodies of unskilled laborers. A modern equivalent waited on the discovery of an equally good binding material. It was found in Portland cement, the use of which increased rapidly in the last years of the nineteenth century and the first of the twentieth. For the superstructure of buildings modern science and economy provided a substitute for the enormous massiveness of Roman concrete. This was the system of reinforcing with iron or steel, first devised in France by Joseph Monier in the 'sixties. A composite structure was thus achieved, strong against both compression and tension, with the steel protected against both rust and fire.

Equally novel in relation to past civilizations were some of the classes of buildings now raised to importance. The railway-station took the place of the old city gate as the point of arrival and departure. In the first stations, in America as in England, the fundamental form was the train shed, which, with the multiplication of tracks and the use of iron arches of great span, acquired a certain beauty—lost, however, in smoke and grime. The development of the "booking-hall," the waiting-room or concourse, gave a more grateful element to emphasize. With the adoption of electric power and the disappearance of the tracks below ground, it became the principal feature, filled with a flowing multitude.

The factory early assumed its fundamental forms—the storied mill for multiplied uniform looms or light machines, the long shed with its traveling crane for heavy manufacturing. When wood was still universal for the upper floors, the striving for security against fire developed a standardized mill construction, with heavy planking on large transverse beams which brought a concentrated weight to the outer walls at short intervals. Economy of structure suggested the concentration of the supports, too, at these points. A range of piers, diminishing as they rose, was the natural resulting form, impressive by its uniformity and length. When concrete replaced brick and wood, the piers spaced themselves more widely; conditions demanded an architectural treatment of novel character and proportion.

[141]

AMERICAN ARCHITECTURE

The sites of American cities on navigable rivers of a size which dwarfs the Thames and the Seine has made their great bridges of steel, high above the masts of ships, striking features in the urban picture. Although at first the work solely of engineers, they operated powerfully on the imagination of architects, as Louis Sullivan has testified, to encourage the use of the new material and stimulate an enfranchisement from traditional constructive forms.

In the old cities of Europe the heights of buildings were officially limited. Early American efforts in this direction were regarded as invasions of the property rights guaranteed by the federal constitution, and for a century there was no other restriction on height than the strength of materials and the willingness to climb stairs. When iron and the elevator came into use in the 'seventies the limit of possibility was raised enormously. Instead of spreading, as in London and Paris and Vienna, buildings, unrestrained by the state, shot upward on the preferred sites. The rentals from many stories increased the value of the land, and, by a circular train of causes, forced neighbors to build higher and higher. The island site of Manhattan, often named as the determining factor, was not so in truth—the incomparable majority of its buildings remained, and still remains, of three and four stories. The most striking early illustration of the tendency, indeed, was not in New York but in Chicago, rebuilding on the vast plain after its great fire.

In the struggle skyward of the first "elevator-buildings," it soon occurred to designers to support the floors entirely on columns of iron, leaving the outer walls with only their own weight to carry. Thus were created such buildings as that of the *World* in New York, with a height of three hundred and seventy-five feet. Here however the self-supporting walls reached a thickness of nine feet, even of twenty or more at some points; the value of the lower stories was compromised. At this moment the decisive step was taken of supporting the wall itself, as well as the floors, on the frame of metal, reducing the wall to a mere veneer or curtain. This was first taken by William Le Baron Jenney in parts of the Home Insurance Building in Chicago, designed in the year 1883 and built from 1884 to 1886.

The economy was vast, the last hindrance to ascent was swept away. William Holabird and Martin Roche, from Jenney's office, used the same scheme throughout their Tacoma Building built in the two following years. These buildings still had cast iron columns and wrought iron beams, but the conception of a continuous steel frame with riveted joints was already present, and the materials were soon available. The sky now became indeed the limit—the skyscraper was born.

These were the economic and constructive developments, of vast import and novelty, by which the stage was set for new creations in form. Not since the Gothic was invented had there been structures so revolutionary. What artistic ideals were to govern them; what character were they to take? Was man to be mastered by the giants of his creation, or to master them? The answer lay with leaders of the generation coming to maturity as the century drew toward its close.

XII

WHAT IS MODERN ARCHITECTURE? THE POLES OF MODERNISM: FUNCTION AND FORM

CHAPTER XII

WHAT IS MODERN ARCHITECTURE?
THE POLES OF MODERNISM:
FUNCTION AND FORM

Two forces struggled for mastery among the men of the 'nineties. One took its impulse from science, the overwhelming power which had dominated the nineteenth century; the other, reacting against science, worked to establish the independence of art. One exalted truth as the supreme principle, in art as in science; the other raised beauty again to independent being. One typified the loving surrender of man to nature; the other, his victory over nature.

The doctrine of truth in art, of obedience to nature, is as old as the ancients. Many a different generation has been able to interpret this as the guiding principle of its own artistic strivings. It was with Herder and Goethe that it took on the meaning it was to have in the nineteenth century. From a model of ordered unity, nature became the source of creative inspiration. The artist, filled with its spirit, in impressing form on his materials, accepts the needs and use, and gives characteristic beauty:

. . . *bis in den kleinsten Theil notwendig schön wie Bäume Gottes.*

The mid-nineteenth century lay under the spell of nature. To the romantic interest was added the scientific. The study of the earth, of plants and animals, culminating in the work of Darwin, gave a new significance to the idea of evolution, as the progressive adaptation of organic form to function and environment. Religion and art alike were influenced by the new concepts. Merit in painting was identified with minute "truth to nature"; beauty in architecture, with truth to use and structure. Keats was the voice of his time when he said, "Beauty is truth, truth beauty."

Frank outward expression of the nature of buildings, of their internal arrangements, and of their construction had, indeed, been characteristic of many earlier styles. As a more conscious principle, purism in the use of structural elements—a rule of "reason" and "good sense"—

had been increasing in French classic architecture since the seventeenth century. Even the Greek revivalists in America, who had masked so many uses and arrangements in the form of the temple, had been careful to limit the column to its original and typical use as an isolated support. At the École des Beaux-Arts, there was indifference to structural suggestions, but the keenest striving to express arrangement and "character."

By the middle of the nineteenth century the demand for "truth" had become insistent. Pugin wrote: "There should be no features about a building which are not necessary for convenience, construction or propriety;" "all ornament should consist of enrichment of the essential construction of the building." Ruskin added a moral fervor of judgment, casting into outer darkness, as "unnatural and monstrous," the styles of Rome and of the Renaissance which he found wanting in structural sincerity. On the Continent Viollet-le-Duc wrote: "There are two ways of expressing truth in architecture; it must fulfil with scrupulous exactness all the conditions imposed by necessity . . . employ materials with due regard for their qualities and capaci-

ties." Semper summed up all in the formula:
"Every technical product a resultant of use and
material."

Evolutionary theory was meanwhile under-
mining the imitation of historic styles from
another side. The principle of national individuality and organic development was applied
in tracing the relation of the art of past schools
to race, environment and time. These ideas
were fundamentally hostile to every "revival" of
historical forms in the modern world.

It was but gradually that they were followed
to their extreme consequences. Pugin and Ruskin and their American disciples still thought
the way of salvation lay through the Gothic for
which they claimed a superiority in truth of expression. Viollet-le-Duc, in spite of his
enthusiasm for the Middle Ages, came ultimately to deny "the propriety of imposing on
our age any reproduction of antique or medieval
forms." Semper announced that "the solution
of modern problems must be freely developed
from the premises given by modernity." He was
himself, however, still content to do his work
with historical elements; and Viollet-le-Duc's at-

tempts to deduce new architectural forms from the sporadic employment of iron in construction had little success. They were too purely cerebral, too little left. We must recognize, also, that the problems and materials currently offered to the designer in 1870 had not yet changed enough from those of previous centuries, or yet crystallized enough to give sufficient basis for a revolutionary change of forms.

A new continent, a new society, a new community, was needed for the realization of "modernist" ideas. In America commercialism, industrial society, had developed unrestrained. Patriotic motives added the call for "American style" to the more general demand for a "modern style."

In the 'seventies and early 'eighties, while the East sought to assimilate itself to cultivated Europe, the West gloried in the American "innocence" exaggerated by Mark Twain. A conjunction especially favorable existed in Chicago. The great fire left a *tabula rasa*—all was to be made new. For once there was an opportunity for young men in that most difficult and responsible of arts, where the "younger

[151]

men" are usually past fifty. On the active and independent spirits who were attracted to the city, the ideas of Viollet-le-Duc and Semper made a deep impression. Van Brunt of Kansas City had translated Viollet's *Discourses;* John Root published excerpts from Semper's work. The Western Association of Architects was founded, with pronounced radical tendencies; a new journal, the *Inland Architect,* gave its sponsors a voice and an audience. There was a ferment of discussion, experiment and emulation.

From the Chicago ferment had come the decisive structural invention, the steel frame carrying the walls as well as the floors. From it, too, before 1890, emerged three men: Daniel Burnham, John Root and Louis Sullivan.

Burnham described himself when he once called another "a dreamer with his feet on the ground." A mystic, alive to beauty and to nature, and with a gift of friendship, he was yet of fixed purpose and immense determination. Great in executive capacity, obsessed with the idea of bigness, of power, he was the architect who grasped the significance of American industrialism, with its vast growth, its organization, its division of labor. It was he who created the type of American architect's office of to-day, with its delegation of responsibility to designers, structural and mechanical engineers, specification writers, superintendents and executives. It was he more than any other to whom the American business building owes its amplitude, its internal clarity of arrangement.

Root, his partner through the years of struggle, was the artist, the designer—magnetic, facile, finished, eager to shine, receptive, enamored of the new. In the race skyward Burnham and Root were in the van; in the struggle for a new form of expression Root was the popular standard-bearer. The decisive structural inventions, however, were not theirs; the inspired artistic creation was made by another.

In Louis Sullivan, Chicago found its poet. Half French, half Irish, he had the analytical mind of a scientist, the soul of a dreamer and artist. Overflowing with romantic enthusiasm for nature, dazzled by the logical splendor of mathematics, fascinated by Taine and Darwin, abased before the titanic creative power of Michelangelo, he had passed rapidly through the discipline of school and of the Beaux-Arts—assimilating, questioning, feeling. At seventeen enamored of Chicago, its energy, its wide horizons of lake and prairie; at twenty-five already established in a position to build his air-castles; at thirty he was a prophet to youth, in lyrical outbursts of rushing words, enveloping an authentic philosophy.

Among the architects of our day, whose expressed notions are apt to be fragments from inconsistent systems, his ideas had an intuitive harmony and value, under "the dominant, all-pervading thought that a spontaneous and vital art must come fresh from nature, and can only thus come." The artist is "to arrest and typify in materials the harmonious and inter-blended rhythms of nature and humanity." To him reason and analysis were not all.

Sensitive, passionate and courageous, he illustrated in his own career that "to the master mind . . . imbued with the elemental significance of nature's moods, humbled before the future and the past, art and its outworkings are largely tragic."

Sullivan's early work, like the work of Root and so many others of less genius, was colored by Richardson's influence. The treatment of the Auditorium Building, with its heavy masonry walls and arches, was suggested by Richardson's design for the Field warehouse. From Richardson must also have come the first suggestion of the foliate ornament which Sullivan afterward developed so characteristically. On the completion of the vast auditorium followed a breakdown, recuperation, a long communing with nature, a gathering of new forces. The return to Chicago in 1890 marks the opening of Sullivan's great creative period.

His first problem was the novel one of the steel-frame office building. The frame must be encased for protection against fire. How might its indispensable presence be expressed? How might the monstrous, unprecedented pile be given artistic form? "He felt at once that the new form of engineering was revolutionary, demanding an equally revolutionary architectural mode. That masonry construction, in so far as tall buildings were concerned, was a thing of the past, to be forgotten, that the mind might be free to face and solve new problems in new functional forms. That the old idea of superimposition must give way before the sense of vertical continuity." So Sullivan wrote in his *Autobiography of an Idea,* a generation later. The Wainwright Building in St. Louis, designed before the close of the year, was the perfect embodiment of this conception.

His own interpretation of the problem formulated most clearly his whole philosophy of art:

"It is my belief that it is of the very essence of every problem that it contains and suggests its own solution. This I believe to be natural law. Let us examine, then, carefully the elements, let us search out this contained suggestion, this essence of the problem. . . .

"Beginning with the first story, we give this a main entrance that attracts the eye to its location, and the remainder of the story we treat in a more or less liberal, expansive, sumptuous way—a way based exactly on the practical necessities, but expressed with a sentiment of largeness and freedom. The second story we treat in a similar way but usually with milder pretension. Above this, throughout the indefinite number of typical office tiers, we take our cue from the individual cell, which requires a window with its separating pier, its sill and lintel, and we, without more ado, make them look all alike because they are all alike. This brings us to the attic,

LATER GOTHIC
The Chapel at West Point

THE STEEL FRAME
The Wainright Building, St. Louis

which, having no division into office cells, and no special requirement for lighting, gives us the power to show by means of its broad expanse of wall, and its dominating weight and character, that which is the fact—namely, that the series of office tiers has come definitely to an end. . . .

"We must now heed the imperative voice of emotion.

"It demands of us, What is the chief characteristic of the tall office building? And at once we answer, it is lofty. This loftiness is to the artist-nature its thrilling aspect. It is the very open organ-tone in its appeal. It must be in turn the dominant chord in his expression of it, the true excitant of his imagination. It must be tall, every inch of it tall. The force and power of altitude must be in it, the glory and pride of exaltation must be in it. It must be every inch a proud and soaring thing, rising in sheer exultation that from bottom to top it is a unit without a single dissenting line—that it is the new, the unexpected, the eloquent peroration of most bald, most sinister, most forbidding conditions. . . .

"The true, the immovable philosophy of the architectural art . . . let me now state, for it brings to the solution of the problem a final, comprehensive formula:

"Whether it be the sweeping eagle in his flight, or the open apple-blossom, the toiling workhorse, the blithe swan, the branching oak, the winding stream at its base, the drifting clouds over all the coursing sun, *form ever follows func-*

tion, and this is the law. Where function does not change, form does not change. . . .

"And thus, when native instinct and sensibility shall govern the exercise of our beloved art . . . when our architects shall cease strutting hand-cuffed and vainglorious in the asylum of a foreign school . . . when we know and feel that Nature is our friend, not our implacable enemy, then it may be proclaimed that we are on the high-road to a natural and satisfying art, an architecture that will soon become a fine art in the true, the best sense of the word, an art that will live because it will be of the people, for the people, and by the people."

In the Wainwright Building, wall surface was abandoned for a system of pier and panel which symbolized the concentrated support of the steel columns. That the terra cotta which gave fire protection was no self-supporting masonry, but a mere casing, was expressed with success by a delicate surface ornament. The height was emphasized by unbroken continuity of the multiplied vertical piers. The building became indeed "every inch a proud and soaring thing," filled with the "force and power of altitude."

In the design Sullivan rose superior to any merely mechanical theory of expression. He achieved unity of form arbitrarily. The steel occurs only at alternate piers, yet all are alike. The artist has felt, not calculated. The building is vitally unified in a form deeply felt by its creator.

Such works emphasized the novel element in modern life, rather than its continuity with the past. Their realistic treatments of its subject matter had an obvious relation with the realistic movements of the nineteenth century in painting and sculpture, in literature and music. Painting from Courbet through the impressionists and neo-impressionists, sculpture in the hands of Carpeaux and Rodin, the music-drama of Wagner, which moved Sullivan so deeply, the novels and plays of Tolstoi, Flaubert, Zola and Ibsen, all consciously sought characteristic beauty through truth to nature, rather than abstract beauty through relations of form. The men of fundamental greatness, indeed, preserved a sense of form in the other arts, as in architecture. The lesser men, however, the imitators— their attention distracted from creation to reproduction—fell into a chaos which we see, for instance, in Monet's successors, where all form is dissolved in light.

[159]

Against this formlessness, this scientific observation of nature, this equation of beauty with truth or half-truth, there had begun, even before 1890, a reaction which was to have far-reaching consequences. Cézanne, still obscure and unregarded, wrote, "All in nature is modeled according to the sphere and the cone and the cylinder," and undertook, as he said, to build a bridge between the impressionists and the Louvre. Scientific anatomy and photographic foreshortening began to give way. In literature Whitman inaugurated a renaissance of verse, with a multitude of novel experiments in form. New leaders in music tended to abandon efforts to express literary ideas and to revert to the pure language of tone, enriched by new scales and harmonies. In this renewed worship of form there was much that emphasized relation to the great past. Ingres and Greco and Bach were hailed and worshiped as moderns.

One of the first of the movements to restore the supremacy of abstract form was gathering force in American architecture in the New York of the late 'eighties. Its standard bearers were McKim, Mead and White. Charles Follen McKim, of Quaker ancestry, austere and delicate in his tastes, with indomitable allegiance to artistic ideals, had been the third American to study at the École des Beaux-Arts. Stanford White, virile and overflowing with energy, reveling in rich materials, in color and ornament, had passed an apprenticeship with Richardson. His tall figure, with red bristling hair, was visible above the crowd in every gay artistic assemblage. Mead, the wise counselor, had been trained in the school at Florence. Of the three, he was the only one who began with a leaning to the classic. The portfolios which McKim and White brought back from France were full of the picturesque high-roofed châteaux which had inspired Hunt. Their first designs used medieval forms. Irregular, romantic dispositions governed their early work, not only in the Queen Anne manner, but in the revived Colonial for which they were the chief sponsors.

Their stimulus to a calmer unity of form came from one of their designers, the gifted and unfortunate Joseph Morrill Wells. On the walls of the office still hang his two sober drawings of the Farnese Palace and of Lescot's wing of the

[161]

Louvre, representing his classic ideals, which became those of his great associates. Although no word of theory ever came from any of them, they must have felt intuitively what a French critic later wrote, that "instead of constructing first, without thinking of the final appearance, promising to use the nature of the construction in the decoration, one should banish the ingenuities of structure among the secondary means, unworthy to appear in the completed work."

Like men in other periods of renewed interest in unity and purity of form, the fifteenth and eighteenth centuries, they turned to the classic, in which the preeminent manifestations of pure or abstract form, as opposed to a structural or plastic emphasis, have doubtless been achieved. Its elements—masses and spaces of geometrical simplicity—offered an established language widely understood.

For this second classic revival there was little stimulus in contemporary Europe. It was American in its origins and was to remain American in its leadership. Although the leaders were men of European training, it was not the style of their French masters which determined theirs. To characteristic emphasis and lavish dynamic energy, they opposed an almost mathematical simplicity, a Dorian harmony. It can scarcely be doubted that the underlying influence must be sought in the heritage of classic monuments from the formative period of the nation which McKim and his associates had been the first to appreciate. Thus the founders of the republic, after a half-century of confusion, once more imposed their artistic ideal.

An interpretation of architecture, as they tacitly conceived it, in terms of mass and space, instead of structure, was indeed to be the theory of the future. Its foundations were laid by German and Italian thinkers independently, but after the first decisive American works. Wells, McKim and White thus led a new van. Their mature work was not merely a belated historical revival, a continuation of the nineteenth century eclecticism, willing to choose between all styles, classic being one. It was rather an affirmation of a different principle of style. It used classic elements, to be sure, but it was not merely imitative. It reaffirmed the supremacy of form, and worked in the classical spirit of unity, uniformity and balance.

The earliest building fully to embody the new

manner was the group of the four Villard houses in New York, built in 1885. No attempt was made to demark or characterize them individually; on the contrary they were welded into a single great palace, simple and uniform. Brownstone, retained as the material over the protests of the architects, was handled with fine feeling. The details were suggested by the Italian Renaissance, with reminiscences of the Cancellaria, but the building was far from being a copy. Its significance lay less in its derivative forms than in its harmonious order and serenity of spirit.

A series of genial works quickly followed. In the Century Club and in Madison Square Garden, on which White and Wells worked together, the Renaissance details were vitalized by a rich flowering of ornament held within simple bounds, and executed in terra cotta with all White's understanding of materials.

Before the close of the decade came McKim's design for the Boston Library. The square mass was unbroken by any projection, the cornice made a continuous bounding line. The long ranks of massive arches were carried blandly, without the

Courtesy of McKim, Mead and White

THE RETURN TO CLASSICAL FORM

The Villard houses, New York

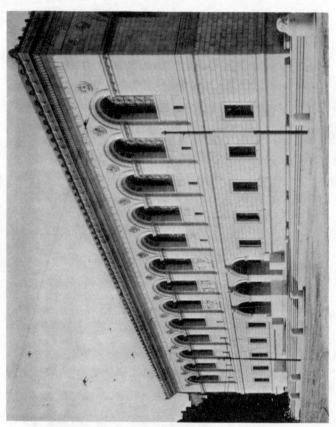

THE MUSIC OF SURFACE
The Boston Public Library

slightest interruption, across the variations of interior use. In Paris Gaudet was saying what a great effect such a uniform front would have by contrast to the Beaux-Arts system of articulation, but there his words fell on unheeding ears. McKim's initiative was independent. The suggestion came to him doubtless from the Library of Ste. Geneviève in Paris, built when France itself was under Greek influence, but the serried proportions of his design, the boldness and depth of relief gave it a different character, a majesty of its own. Inside, the same harmony prevailed, with a richness and sobriety of sculptured and painted decoration which was new in America.

The battleground of the two forces, for the supremacy between form and function between East and West, was the World's Fair of 1893. Chicago, which had won the preliminary contest between cities for the privilege of holding the fair, was eagerly alive to its opportunity. But twenty years from a day when it lay in ashes, it was to justify before the world its aspiration to be a world metropolis, a center of civilization and art as well as of trade. The fair was to body forth this dream.

At first it was thought that the whole work might be given to Burnham and Root. The time was too short. Burnham became Chief of Construction. Root, as consulting architect, began studies to determine the general character of the buildings. These already show an intention to abandon the conservatory aspect of the older expositions, and to suggest permanent buildings—a dream city. They were of a free style, with some recognition of the steel construction, but still reminiscent of Richardson's Romanesque.

Meanwhile the architects had been appointed for the individual buildings—five from the East, five from the West. On the eve of their meeting came the death of Root. Many have speculated on what might have been the outcome had he lived. It is doubtful whether it would have been very different. Burnham was already dazzled by the prestige of the Eastern men, whose common training in the Beaux-Arts tradition inclined them to a formal plan, to unity of the ensemble, and to classic rather than free or medieval forms. They made common cause, while the Western men aimed at personal variety. It was thus not wholly arbitrary that the central group, closely knit, fell to the Easterners, the outer buildings, scattered among the greenery and the lagoons, to the Western men. The central group became a Court of Honor, to which the designers, throwing aside their preliminary sketches where each had sought to outdo the other, quickly agreed to give a uniform cornice, a uniform brilliant whiteness, and a general congruity of style, the classic. The sheds of steel and wood disappeared behind majestic colonnaded fronts. Within the diversity which this still allowed, McKim's building, suggestive of the Roman baths, with vast columns rising from ground to cornice, was the one to captivate the beholders.

The Westerners, with a single exception, ranged freely among the historic styles. Sullivan was the only man to seek a novel expression. Still permeated with subtler historical reminiscences—Roman, Romanesque and Moorish—his Transportation Building was given a character of its own by its wealth of color, its rich flowering of original ornament about the vast Golden Doorway.

Burnham, keen in his judgment of trends and of men, took as his own designer, in place of Root, Charles Attwood of New York, who seized on McKim's Roman style, and even outdid him in simplicity, in breadth, and in beauty of proportion. Attwood's great peristyle toward the lake, his Palace of the Fine Arts, mirrored in the lagoon, were of unforgettable dignity and grandeur.

The cumulative impression of the classic phantasm was overwhelming. The throng of visitors, many of whom were seeing large buildings for the first time, was deeply stirred by the ordered magnificence and harmony of the Court of Honor. The example of unified effort and effect, associated with the classic forms in which it had been achieved, was stamped on the memory of the whole nation.

The issue, whether function should determine form from within or whether an ideal form might be imposed from without, had been decided for a generation by a sweeping victory for the formal ideal.

XIII

THE TRIUMPH OF CLASSICAL FORM

CHAPTER XIII

THE TRIUMPH OF CLASSICAL FORM

THE effect of the Chicago Fair was electric. American architecture turned to the formal, the classical, the monumental. A Roman grandeur now replaced Italian delicacy and the luxuriance of the first works.

Coming in the teeth of the hostile reigning theory of function, the work of McKim and his associates was indeed at first attacked as arbitrary and even as false. The public, however, was quick to respond to the basic appeal of groups of unified and dominated masses, to the musical compositions of interior space. Other architects, often still mouthing an opposite inherited theory, were borne along by the new current.

Although, to many of the later works of the school, the École des Beaux-Arts contributed its analytical science and virtuosity of planning, it is mistaken to suppose the movement itself to be,

[171]

as Jacques Gréber has asserted, *"preuve de la force d'expansion du génie français."* The scores of students who have returned from the unrivaled discipline and emulation of the Paris school, have had here to lay aside their French language of form, and learn anew a language which had been that of their greatest ancestors. Not one has permanently escaped the influence of the American classic.

Using the Roman alphabet, the established universal terms of classical form, the American designers made what had been thought a dead language the idiom of current speech, expressing with unexpected flexibility the ideas of a new age. To a degree unknown in a century of Babel, they made it common to the whole body of designers and workmen, who thus could easily understand one another all over a great continent. They were able to work forward in common effort. A coherent body of tradition was again established. As in the old days before wide historical knowledge, the artist stood on the shoulders of his forerunners. The general nature of his work established, he felt not bound, but free to vary, develop and refine his utterance. In the sympathetic study of the elements themselves, of profiles, of color, of departures from mechanical regularity through curvature and inclination, of the problems arising in adaptation to new uses, to a new and vaster scale, he felt he had a sufficient field for his creative powers.

McKim and his fellows went on from triumph to triumph, finding in the early buildings of the Republic a supporting tradition and a national sanction.

The city of Washington, since the early days, had grown with little direction. At the turn of the century, the men who had made the White City in Chicago were summoned to outline the development of the national capital. Serious changes had been made in the original plan; errors generally felt to be beyond repair. L'Enfant's Mall, which was to make a long formal vista westward from the Capitol, had been planted by Downing as a romantic landscape park with winding roads, and trees, irregularly disposed, already grown tall. Squarely across it lay the tracks of a great railroad terminal. The Washington Monument, which was to have stood where the vistas of Capitol and White House crossed, had been located, for better foundations, neither just on the one line nor on the other.

Burnham and McKim, who with Olmsted the younger and the sculptor St. Gaudens formed the Park Commission, took the bravest and simplest way. In spite of all obstacles, they restored L'Enfant's plan. Under Burnham's persuasion the railroad abandoned its devastating central site. The western vista was boldly pointed fair at the Monument, ignoring squareness. Beyond a terrace to the west, a pool, a vast circular mirror, marked the crossing of the southern vista from the White House. L'Enfant's plan had gone no farther west or south. The Monument in his plan had stood on the marshy bank of the Potomac. With the same courage L'Enfant had shown in planning beyond his day, the new commissioners extended his lines far out over the tidal flats. Thus they created at the outer ends two new monumental sites of the first importance. They destined one for a Lincoln Memorial, the other for a shrine to the founders of the republic. The suggested forms harmonized yet contrasted with those of

[174]

the Capitol, the White House and the Monument.

The government buildings, since the Civil War, had run the gamut of materials and of historic styles. The commissioners now proposed a return to the calm and uniform classic of the founders. The White House had been defaced by conservatories without; within, Victorian overstuffing and screens of painted glass had given it the character of a Pullman car or a river steamboat. For its enlargement two overshadowing circular pavilions had recently been proposed. McKim swept away the outer excrescences, restored Jefferson's lateral colonnades, and subordinated the new offices at the end. Inside, if he did not fully achieve the character of the original work, still imperfectly understood, he at least returned to consonant classical forms. New government buildings established not only the proposed lines on the Mall, but the intended, quiet, formal character of the whole setting for the focal monuments.

The Park Commission had no autocratic authority. Its designs were backed by little greater power than their own persuasive force.

They have been able to withstand every on-
slaught, and to-day, after a generation, are established in their essentials. They justified Burnham's prophetic insight when he said, in his
finest utterance: "Make no little plans. They
have no magic to stir men's blood, and probably
themselves will not be realized. Make big plans,
aim high in hope and work, remembering that a
noble and logical diagram, once recorded will
never die, but long after we are gone will be a
living thing, asserting itself with ever growing insistence. . . . Let your watchword be order
and your beacon, beauty."

In San Francisco, in Chicago, in the distant
Philippines, Burnham led the way in an imaginative reincarnation of the cities. Chicago discovered its lake and its rivers. Along the front
it created its endless drives and lagoons, projected its civic forum dominating a vast man-
made harbor. New York put the railway under
ground, and above, created Park Avenue with
its colossal uniform buildings. Philadelphia,
awaking to its vast wealth, boldly broke its Parkway through a neglected quarter from the center
to the Schuylkill at Fairmount. It has crowned

this acropolis with a great temple of the arts, and is lining the way to its foot with the new homes of its venerable institutions of culture.

The reaction against romanticism, evident in these great works of town planning, was equally influential in the design of estates and houses. White had early reverted to the formal garden, which was soon to find a master in Charles Platt. A painter-etcher, saturated with the garden-craft of Italy, he made, for his friends of St. Gaudens' artistic colony at Cornish, gardens which made his services everywhere in demand. From gardens and their decorative structures it was an easy step to houses and estates treated as a single whole. Broad terraces with steps and fountains, walled parterres with hedges, statuary and quiet pools were his elements for an intimate union of architecture and sculpture, of water and vegetation. Sometimes the forms of detail were Italian, as in the Harold McCormick place at Lake Forest, with its terraces above the lake; sometimes they were suggested by early American precedents as in Eastover, or the Manor House at Glen Cove. Always they were tranquil, balanced, serene. These qualities, shared with the works of the first leaders of the movement, dominated in the work of Pope, of Delano and Aldrich, and others who now joined in establishing the tone of domestic architecture. The magnificent ostentation of the 'eighties gave place to an easy refinement, a reserved elegance.

In monumental buildings the favorite motives of the early Republic came again to honor. The banks reverted to the models of Latrobe, endlessly varied. For the largest of them, the National City, McKim took the old New York Merchants Exchange, and placed a Corinthian story above its great Ionic front. Its long colonnade, with that of the old Treasury, gave suggestions for the front of the vast New York Post Office and many another work. A Roman triumphal arch, such as Bulfinch had erected to celebrate Washington's inauguration, was built by White for the centenary of that event, and made permanent in marble. Mills' tall Greek Doric column became the model for McKim's monument to the martyrs of the Prison Ships and for the memorial of Perry's victory on Lake Erie.

The ordered form and classic spirit of the University of Virginia, which McKim and White were soon to restore after fire, gave the suggestion for their academic groups at Columbia and New York Universities. In each a great library, with low massive dome, dominated a balanced court of sober related buildings. Rarely have there been finer conceptions of the centralized vaulted hall than in these two rotundas, one square below with four vast arches and colonnades, the other a perfect circle, with a single continuous ring of columns, an unbroken overarching hemisphere. The austerity of one, the richness of the other, glowing with bronze and gold, reflected the personalities of McKim and of White, here matched one against the other in friendly emulation.

The domed church, of the type Mills had chosen for the evangelical sects, suggested itself again to White, when he had to build for the Presbyterians in Madison Square. His task was indeed discouraging. The site was surrounded by high commercial structures; on the opposite corner was soon to rise the highest building in the world. Any conventional church tower would have been trivial and ineffective. He chose a solid cubical mass with a low dome, a colossal portico of polished granite, as overpowering by its vast scale as the neighboring structure was by its height. As always with White, the materials and textures were given a rich and masterly treatment.

Lingering scruples long prevented the bodily imitation of the temple, but fruitful suggestions were found in other antique types, unregarded in earlier days. The peristyle, completely surrounding the building, reappeared in John Russell Pope's Temple of the Scottish Rite at Washington, a superb restudy of the motive of the ancient Mausoleum. The square mass rising above the broad simple terraces of approach, the colonnade with its perfect uniformity every way, the centralizing pyramid above, unite in an effect of overwhelming simplicity and grandeur.

A design of unique brilliance, embodying in extreme form the classic ideal of unity, won for Guy Lowell the competition for the New York Court House. The site, an irregular polygon, the many similar court rooms required, made the problem one of great difficulty. Practical and artistic conditions alike were satisfied in the form conceived by Richmond, one of Lowell's designers—a perfect circle, with a ring of courtrooms, story above story, round a circular waiting hall. It was a type of mass which had not been adopted since the building of Hadrian's great monument in Rome, of which the core survives in the Castle of St. Angelo. The war intervened to delay the execution and increase the cost. Economy then dictated the abandonment of the circular form for a hexagonal one, still notable in its crystalline quality.

A perfect realization of the classic ideal was reached in the Lincoln Memorial in Washington. The struggle which preceded its building showed that the conceptions of the artistic leaders had been firmly grasped by some of the controlling figures of public life. Against the other romantic sites proposed, it held its place of honor on the main axis. McKim had shown there an oblong temple-like peristyle, placed across the line of the vista, sheltering a colossal statue of the savior of the Union. This scheme was retained by Henry Bacon—one of McKim's artistic heirs with a Greek sensitiveness and refinement all his own—who was entrusted with the work. A long canal bordered with straight avenues was led from the obelisk to the foot of vast circular terraces which uphold the pedestal. A wall within the surrounding columns was raised above in a simple attic, carved with emblems of all the states. Inside, facing the Capitol, from which one approaches, is the great brooding figure of Lincoln. On the walls of pillared recesses to left and right are graved the noble words of his two immortal utterances. There is nothing more, except the supreme distinction and peace of the architectural forms themselves, handled with love and refinement by an artist of quiet and choice spirit. There is no effort, other than in the statue, specifically to characterize the individual—the uncouthness of the rustic vanishes in the nobility of the man—his greatness in the life of the nation is marked by the dominance of the site, the grandeur of the scale.

Along with these achievements in simplicity of mass went a renewed solicitude for form in interior space. The elementary geometrical shapes of sphere and cylinder were variously combined in vast vaulted halls. In the banks, the exchanges, the railway-stations they symbolized the majesty of finance and of commerce.

THE TRIUMPH OF CLASSICAL FORM—The Court of Honor, Chicago

From "Manhattan, the Magical Island," courtesy of Ben Judah Lubschez

THE MUSIC OF SPACE
The Pennsylvania waiting room, New York

TRIUMPH OF CLASSICAL FORM

The lofty waiting-room of the Pennsylvania Station in New York takes its suggestion from the fabrics of imperial Rome. The construction of steel is but a hidden means to achieve a grandiose scenic effect. The practical functions of the room, too, are insignificant. It is conceived, rather, in accordance with its higher, ideal function—as a civic vestibule to the world metropolis. In the soaring, musical spaces, the spirit of the newcomer is exalted, to evoke in him a new ambition, a new power.

The immense terminal concourse of the Grand Central, with its multitudinous unceasing life, its sheer towering supports upholding the blue vault strewn with the signs of the heavens, is the image of the modern cosmos.

In the design of tall buildings, Sullivan's expression of altitude by accenting the vertical lines long imposed itself, not only on the few who, like him, sought to abandon inherited forms, but on their antagonists. For a score of years it held undisputed sway in this, its first province. Even men who were content to choose here and there among the historic styles, gave at least lip source to "structural expression." When Woolworth called on Cass Gilbert to surpass all other buildings in height, he turned for precedent to the Gothic, with its soaring lines, and raised a cathedral of commerce. Even the most consistent devotees of abstract form and of classical balance did not remain untouched by these examples. In their New York Municipal Building, their first true skyscraper, McKim, Mead and White marked the lines of the steel columns by shallow vertical strips. Above, an arbitrary abstract form, a circular crown of columns, contrasted with the structural expression below.

Even the skyscraper, the very stronghold of the defenders of functional expression, was ultimately to be captured, at least for a moment, by the champions of form. Their victory came in the building of the Century Holding Company, the first of the "millionaire apartments" built on Fifth Avenue shortly before the war. Here McKim and his associates no longer compromised, but were true to their own implicit theory of form. The steel frame disappeared behind tall curtain walls of unbroken masonry, the merits of which lay in uniformity, rhythm and proportion. Almost simultaneously rose

TRIUMPH OF CLASSICAL FORM

Platt's Leader-News Building in Cleveland with its vast plane surfaces of grooved stone. To the vertical lines of Sullivan's high buildings, identical with them in mass, they opposed horizontal belts and horizontal lines. To the suggestion of the serried trunks of the forest they opposed that of the sheer cliff of bedded stone, equally impressive in its loftiness.

The multitude of high apartment buildings east of Central Park followed the new example with one accord. The Federal Reserve Bank raised its vast precipices in the narrow canyons down-town. For better or for worse, the struggle to express the steel frame, so crucial in the 'nineties, became a dead issue.

The effect of the new formalism was widely felt abroad. The French, who made fun of the colonnades at Chicago in 1893, recalled them in the Paris Exposition of 1900, so unlike all its European predecessors. The English, abandoning the traditions of Ruskin, became frank in admiration. The leaders of the new generation there, like Adshead, Richardson and Atkinson, came to know America well. With a stimulated appreciation of form they strove to base a new

[185]

development on their own fine classic architecture of 1800. Lutyens, at the height of his career, abandoned the medieval tradition and sought to assimilate the classic spirit. The theatric baroque of Wren, which had lived on in the "free classic" of Belcher and in the later work of Norman Shaw, tended to give way to a quieter and more tempered speech. When Harvey Corbett built Bush House in the Strand, the first great American work on English soil, the chorus of tongues in admiration of its boldness and simplicity showed how complete was the revolution in English taste. In the British colonies American influence was great: the architecture of Canada, Australia and New Zealand became predominantly American in its style. An urge to simplicity and clarity of form made itself felt all over the world.

McKim and his associates were eager to perpetuate their style by other means besides stone. With the eternal hope of elder generations, running counter to the endless creative renewal of art, they labored to found institutions which should be the guardians of their established order. At a great dinner in Washington McKim

Courtesy of McKim, Mead and White

THE POLES OF MODERNISM

The Guaranty (Prudential) Building, Buffalo

Apartments for the Century Holding Company, New York

OLD MATERIAL AND NEW FORM
The Wainright tomb, St. Louis

brought together the heads of state and church to establish and sanctify the supremacy of classic form. The Commission of Fine Arts was created to defend the plans for Washington; the American Academy in Rome to crown the education of youth; the American Academy of Art and Letters to recognize and dignify the elders. All seemed fair as the war interrupted for a moment the prodigious activity in building.

XIV

COUNTER-CURRENTS

CHAPTER XIV

COUNTER-CURRENTS

AT THE height of the classical flood, Louis Sullivan, aged and defeated but still undaunted, refused to believe his ship had sunk but spoke of it as a submarine. It did, indeed, continue to move beneath the surface, borne on by an undercurrent.

Sullivan still worked, although the great commissions in the West fell increasingly to others, who adopted the reigning taste. The Wainwright tomb, cubical and domed, with strong simple bands of characteristic ornament, gates and doors freshly imagined, is perhaps the most significant of his later designs. His little banks, conceived as an expression of the strong box, lack the magisterial conviction of the Wainwright Building. He found in them no vitally new problem, no new construction, to bear him up. When he had again to do with steel, in the Guaranty or Prudential Building in Buffalo, he repeated the formulæ of the Wainwright Building with little modification. Thus, in the phrase of his chief artistic heir, Sullivan remained essentially a man of one building.

The spirit of freedom from historic precedent, or at least of freedom in using it, persisted to a certain degree in the work of many Chicago architects. Pond at Hull House and elsewhere, Perkins in his schools, Howard Shaw in his country houses, were but a few of those who strove for a new idiom. Some of their buildings, like Shaw's Bartlett house at Lake Geneva, with its garden court, are of much beauty. Consciously or unconsciously, historical reminiscence still played a great rôle in them. Neither in the elements nor in the dispositions were they fundamentally and richly creative.

A single figure of genius emerged in the generation after Sullivan: Frank Lloyd Wright, Sullivan's favorite helper, who had from the beginning the force to rise above imitation and discipleship. Thoroughly grounded in engineering, he had, not less than Sullivan, the soul of a lover and an artist. A reader of Goethe, he too was a worshiper of nature.

His first work, the Winslow house, built in the year of the Chicago Fair, already shows elements of his mature style, developed in the houses of following years, with conscious adaptation to the wide horizons of the prairie. The plan is flexible, ramified, unsymmetrical, built up exclusively of rectangular elements, with each practical subdivision segregated, each wing, each room separately projected into the gardens and into the landscape. On the exterior, the effect is of repeatedly interrupted and again continued masses, of shifting planes, of severe horizontalism gained by rows of small windows closely beneath an immensely projecting, continuous roof of gentle slope. The wall is gathered into isolated piers. The joints of the brickwork are deeply shadowed to accentuate still more the horizontal effect. Inside there is again the horizontal, in the low ceiling, the strong lines of its construction, the wide-stretched, heavy brick fireplace. Structural features, newly conceived, are everywhere emphasized, in the furnishings as well as in the building. Outside and in, the only decoration, often, is the living flower, in long stone troughs under the windows, in square bowls

[193]

on the terraces and gate piers, in vases continually renewed. The style appears in its perfection in the Coonley house and in Wright's own place, Taliesin, twice destroyed by man and nature, twice rebuilt with unquenchable courage.

His writings, hymning nature and science, have emphasized the organic aspect of modern art as an outgrowth of changing practical problems, of new materials. From the beginning, he welcomed the machine as the tool of modernity, superseding the old handicraft. But a single industrial building has fallen to him, in which these ideas could find full expression—the Larkin Building in Buffalo, for the administration of a great factory, set in a district laid waste by crass industrialism. There is an astonishingly apt conception of the problem in all its practical terms: the absence of outlook, the pollution of the outer air, the need of light, of inner supervision and order, the desire to standardize and mechanize. The interior is treated as a single cubical void, subdivided indeed by slender supports for the storied galleries which look inward on a long central court. The windows to the outer day are high-silled and broad, filling all

NEW USE AND NEW FORM
The Larkin factory, Buffalo

NEW MATERIAL AND NEW FORM
Unity Temple, Oak Park

the width from pier to pier. They are not for view and air, but to let in the light of the sky. The building breathes through the top by vast ducts at the corners. The executives, seated in the midst among their staff, overlook the whole area. The recurrent desks and files, lamps and dictaphones, make the sole adornment, except that from the upper gallery, devoted to refreshment, flowers look down. On the exterior the organization is one of mass. Every accessory element is used to make projection, and to create a three-dimensional effect.

In the same way Wright has sought to analyze and to feel the characteristic ideal and practical requirements, as well as the novel structural aspects, of each problem he has attacked. "Architecture," he has said, "is the Idea of the thing—made to sing to heaven." In his church, the Unity Temple at Oak Park, the cubical interior with its four equal arms with tiers and galleries, its staircases in the angles, gives rise to the outwardly cubical articulated mass. The material, concrete, cast in temporary wooden molds, suggests the box-like form of the walls, the simple slab of the roofs. The whole building is a monolith. The Imperial Hotel at Tokio is again a monolith of concrete, cast this time in permanent molds of brick and lava, with roofs and balconies overhanging on a cantilever principle. The ornament is of geometrical abstraction, not a leaf is carved, though living leaves grow everywhere. Nature, so loved and studied by the designer, who foresaw her angry as well as her smiling moods, has respected his work. In the vast upheaval of the earth which engulfed the city, it alone survived.

In spite of their conscious rationale, Wright, in all these works, has remained unconsciously the romantic artist. Their effort toward "expression," their exaggeration of the characteristic, binds them, in spite of the novelty of their forms, to the great romantic tradition. Romantic too are the reminiscences of older forms, from exotic cultures of the East, which still survive in his imagination and in his buildings.

An independent initiative in the design of industrial buildings was taken by Ernest Wilby, associated with Albert Kahn of Detroit, not long after the Larkin Building. The adoption of reinforced concrete had spaced the piers of factories more widely, without as yet affecting their conventional exterior design. Their small windows still limited the width of storied mills. In the building of the first great Ford plant at Highland Park, the idea came of filling the whole space from pier to pier with glass, held by steel sash of a new type, flooding the stories with daylight. In contrast with the old mill construction the effect was strongly horizontal. The concrete frame could itself be exposed; the wall abandoned except for a low parapet below the window sills. Thus arose a new type of factory, expressive of the new construction. There were practical advantages: economy of material, greater effective width which could be adequately lighted. Almost overnight the scheme was adopted in thousands of American plants, and foreign imitation soon followed.

The steel sash, strong enough to be self-supporting over large areas, soon came to have other applications. In foundries and power houses of a single high story, with traveling cranes supported on steel, all the side of the great shed could now readily be made of glass, without any interruption by intermediate posts. The whole physiognomy of industrial buildings was quite changed.

The brilliant beginning has, indeed, scarcely been followed up in America; Wilby himself felt that, with all the expressiveness, beauty had not been attained. The first schemes evolved by the architects were of such obvious availability that they were quickly seized on by engineers, who alone are consulted in most American industrial work, and applied as formulæ with little further artistic development.

Wright's direct followers in America have too often, as he has complained, taken the letter for the spirit. The idea of an "organic architecture" was not understood, but the forms in which he clothed it were ignorantly copied, cheapened and debased. About Chicago and through the West, his "Prairie style" in houses had descended, before the war, even to the jerry-builder, eager only for a popular catch-word. Few of his pupils have had the strength to stand alone. Walter Burley Griffin, indeed, was victor in competition for the plan of Canberra, the capital of federal Australia, but his work in that far continent has scarcely risen above the horizon.

With Wright himself in exile, the movement he led came to a standstill in Chicago and America, its forces disintegrating.

His voice, so little heeded in his own country, has meanwhile echoed around the world. It found foreign listeners prepared. The same forces of life and thought which brought it forth in America, were beginning to call forth related expressions in the Europe of the 'nineties. Soon after Sullivan's pioneer achievement, Hankar and Horta in Belgium were laying the foundations for *l'art nouveau,* with its curved lines suggestive of plant forms, which flourished among the French craftsmen without at first greatly affecting architecture.

It is in Germany that the rebellion against historical forms, the Secession, has had the widest success. In Vienna Otto Wagner demanded that "modern art must yield us modern ideas, forms created by us, which represent our abilities, our acts, and our preferences." He, too, recognized and welcomed the advent of the machine. Peter Behrens in Berlin found a fertile field of experiment in the power houses and factories of modern industry. A new generation has sprung up, since 1900, of men who no longer think in historic terms. "Organic," the single word of praise which Albert Einstein gave Erich Mendelsohn, the architect of his unique laboratory, may stand as their watchword, as it was that of Sullivan, and is that of Wright. Taking their suggestion at first from science, the German designers have moved, since Cézanne's revolution in painting, toward a more purely artistic unity of form.

In Germany, in Scandinavia, in Holland, in the countries on the Slavic frontier, the name of Wright is one to conjure with. It was in Germany that his drawings were first sumptuously published; in Holland the leaders have united in a splendid tribute. On the other side of the world, the Japanese, after the earthquake, wanted him to take charge of the rebuilding of Tokio. At home his design for a skyscraper remains unbuilt. The influence of his ideas here is indirect.

XV

THE PRESENT

CHAPTER XV

THE PRESENT

WITH the close of the Great War, building, rudely but briefly interrupted, began anew, with even greater energy. Superficially all was much as before. The established order, the supremacy of classical form, continued, not without vitality for new growth. In the composition of mass in high buildings it has discovered a new field of achievement. Nevertheless, it is threatened with more than one danger, within and without.

Chief of these is a certain loss of momentum. Like every other artistic cycle, it had its initial stimulus, its great leaders able by the freshness of their ideals to give new form to all they touched, its army of disciples, following out this or that path merely broken by their masters, its gradual subjugation of a whole territory. Some day must come when there are no new worlds to conquer. When a régime has become settled it is always its weaknesses which are obvious, and it

[203]

is then, not in the moment of victory, that they begin to tell. There is then a weakening of the first impetus, a fatigue of the adherents, who begin to drop away. Ultimately comes a moment when the eager spirit of youth is in open rebellion. For the classic cycle in America such a time may be long hence—the conquest is too recent—but signs of inner exhaustion are not wanting.

From the side of classicism most of the great problems of our time have been attacked and solved with such perfect conformity to its ideals that little room is left for further creative effort in the same direction. In dealing with these problems the disciples of McKim are condemned to ring the changes on the models already established. These tend to harden into formulæ, sometimes relieved in their application by subtle restudy of proportion and detail.

In the effort to vary them there is to-day a recrudescence of the old eclecticism, the choice of other languages and dialects of historic style. Generally these have been ones bordering on the classic—the suggestion, for instance, has been Byzantine or Romanesque, with a strong clas-

THE CATHEDRAL OF MAMMON

Woolworth Building,
New York

THE ARROW
Bush Tower, New York

sical tinge. Renewed experiments have not been wanting, however, with the forms of styles more sharply distinct, like the Gothic. This experimental trend is clearly visible in the work of Harvey Corbett. He has striven to achieve new values within the classic tradition, as in his Springfield civic group of two isolated cubical masses with a campanile between, or in his Masonic memorial at Alexandria with its tall tower of receding columned stages. He has turned also to Gothic as in the arrow-like Bush tower, and to other, freer media, as in the tower at One Fifth Avenue. There is in this no attempt to change the basic ideals, but only the struggle for creative opportunity, on the part of an artist who has reaffirmed his faith in them by saying, "I have only one God: beauty of form."

This diversity has been emphasized by the individualism of religious sects, which has extended from creeds to the church fabrics themselves. Only in the newer cults, like Christian Science, has White's initiative of a domed auditorium of monumental classic form been widely adopted. The other Protestant sects have generally preferred to emphasize their early establishment: the evangelical, by reversion to the Colonial; the Anglican by adherence to the Gothic. In the Anglican Cathedral of St. John the Divine in New York, the initial Romanesque scheme has later been revised into Gothic, which even Burnham was led to believe in for the style of the cathedral at Washington. Catholicism has found in the Roman basilica a reconciliation between its old traditions and the supremacy of classical form.

In the building of houses, local tradition has been the most powerful force. In the original seaboard states, Colonial example has been observed more closely, and its provincial varieties have become the bases of diverse local developments in New England, in the "Dutch Colonial" area around New York, in the ledge-stone region of Pennsylvania, in the Virginia Piedmont. In Louisiana, the unique style of the old buildings, with its French suggestions, has not been without influence. In New Mexico the primitive adobe construction has found notable application. Most conspicuous has been the following of Spanish suggestions, enriched with elements from other semitropic countries, in Florida and Southern California. In all these phases of inherited classic style a great simplicity of character has been held in common.

Counter to the overwhelming popular interest in antique Colonial "Americana," there has been, nevertheless, an increasing tendency among architects to eschew the use of any pronounced historic forms, and to depend on the loving study of textures and on gifted individual craftsmen in the allied arts. In this vein, artists like Harrie Lindeberg, Lewis Albro and Arthur Meigs have achieved personal results of much quiet beauty.

Proselytes more whole-souled in their conversion from adherence to precedent have not been wanting. The most distinguished was Bertram Goodhue. In his best years, when still in the prime of life, he abandoned Gothic and classic alike, and was struggling to find a new mode of expression. In the competition for the great war memorial in Kansas City he met a reformed classicist of similar tendencies, Van Buren Magonigle. Their designs had much in common—vast blocklike masses with sculptural enrichment, colonnades reduced to lowest terms, in which only the suggestion and the proportions were classical. In Goodhue's, the chief element was a background for colossal sculptured figures, recalling somewhat the massive German monuments of the imperial period. Magonigle's, now in course of execution, was the simpler and more impressive. A tall circular buttressed shaft, visible for leagues over the prairie, rises from an immense platform of masonry, flanked by two low cubical structures. The simplicity of motive, the contrast between upright and level on a vast scale, is of elemental power.

For the capitol of Nebraska, Goodhue used a similar composition—a square tower of extreme height rising from the plain, in the midst of a vast square low mass, of the utmost architectural nudity. Four arms of a great cross rise slightly above the outer enclosing mass, and give the tower visual support. Although medieval reminiscences are everywhere, and the idea of the tower itself is a romantic conception, the classic spirit of symmetry and uniformity prevails in the treatment of surfaces and spaces. The fusion is not entirely complete. We may welcome the experiment, but we must recognize that the new hybrid still recalls somewhat too insistently its diverse origins.

The same disinfected classicism prevails in Goodhue's last work, the building of the American Academy of Sciences in Washington. Downcast at first at the requirement of conformity to the established character of the surroundings, he strove to vitalize the old formulæ by elimination of columnar elements, by refinement of profiling and restraint of sculptured ornament. In spite of its beauty of material and detail, the building suffers from the breaks in the simple rhythm of its façade. The forms but not the spirit of the classic are there. In these later works Goodhue's achievement is more of a negative than a positive character. He has tried to expurgate without bringing much that is deeply creative.

Beside such internal movements, a reflux from abroad is favoring the drift from the classic. Certain American artists have recognized the creative liberty secured by the Germans, and are trying to free themselves from the bondage of academic detail while preserving the American heritage of simplicity and unity of form. Thus it is, for instance, with Clarence Zantzinger and Charles Borie of Philadelphia. In their earlier work on the Philadelphia Museum of Art, the refinements of form and the splendors of color have shown that the purest classic may still have vitality. In their Fidelity Mutual Building, on the other hand, without the slightest effect of the bizarre which would betray an exotic element, the simple forms have freed themselves from the chilling hand of precedent. The irregular site has been handled brilliantly to produce an unusual balanced composition. The two immense arched portals contrast with the long ranges of simple piers. Rich sculpture and color and gilding enhance the effect.

Another impulse from abroad was given by the Paris exposition of decorative arts in 1925, where surviving elements of the *art nouveau,* which had remained in solution, were precipitated by reagents from Vienna. Under the intelligent fostering of Charles Richards, American manufacturers were interested, and experiment with new forms has begun again in American interiors and furnishing.

The recrudescence of materialism which has followed the war has thrown the preponderance in American architecture on commercial structures and other buildings for investment. The unparalleled abundance of public, monumental building in the preceding period is not approached in the vastly greater total volume of construction to-day. The tall office building with steel frame is again in the center of interest. By itself this has given a new stimulus to fresh adventure.

The direction which this has taken was powerfully affected by the provisions of the ordinance adopted in New York during the war to regulate the height of buildings. This law, while arbitrarily limiting the general height of wall on the street line in different regions or zones of the city, allowed certain portions of the wall to exceed this height, permitted walls to rise still higher in proportion as they were set back from the street, and placed no limitation of height on a tower which should occupy not more than one-quarter of the site. Some of these provisions recognized tendencies already evident. The advantages of outlook and light had already led often to the abandonment of inner for outer courts, deeply indenting the front, and modeling the upper part of long façades with comb-like teeth. In the race for height, with its advantages of réclame, it had already proved less costly to carry skyward but a part of the whole building. The Singer Tower, the Metropolitan Tower, and the Woolworth Tower, which had successively outrivaled all others, had given the suggestion. The other clauses of the law now encouraged further departures from the single cubical mass usual in the early office buildings.

In many structures of mere utility, the legal provisions have been allowed to have their effect mechanically without the effort to fuse and recast the form in the creative spirit. Some of these raw novel products of law and economics, like the buildings of the Garment Center, with their vast bulk stepped in receding stories, already show elements of style, and achieve a new aspect.

In the hands of the artistic leaders the crude masses have fallen into order. It is with the sculpturing of mass, hitherto always possible but little regarded in the higher buildings, that they are now concerned. Surface and detail have become less significant. The towers thrust themselves upward, bastioned all about. In their grouping there is an infinitude of possibilities. It matters little whether every foot of cubic space within the legal "envelope" is filled. Volume for volume desired, the steel frame may as easily be high as broad. The air above is free to enclose. Already these varied opportunities are being avidly seized. Among the new works daily taking form are certain masterly creations.

In the Shelton Hotel, the work of Arthur Loomis Harmon, the tower stands broadside to the street. From the front, the building seems not merely to have a tower, but to be a tower. In three great leaps of rhythmic height it rises, gathering in its forces for the final flight. The vertical files of rooms, alternately projected, leave shallow recesses, making tall upright lines which continue uninterrupted into the silhouette against the sky. At the top, the great windows of the pool terminate the uniform underlying pattern of the small openings below. Faint touches of Italian Romanesque detail are insignificant in the essential freshness of conception.

In the great office building, broader and lower,

built by Ely Jacques Kahn at the foot of Park Avenue, there are only three simple masses, three diminishing cubes, the upper ones distinguished by broad use of color. The staged tower of the Babylonians comes again to life.

Here and in the Shelton all is rectangular, cubical. In the Fraternity Clubs, solids of other forms appear, octagonal and circular. The use of masses other than the cubical had already been suggested in the crowns of the Municipal and Bush Towers; now the enrichment of form is carried into the outer supporting blocks.

Tht Ritz Tower shoots upward like a slender arrow. On one of the most valuable sites in the world, its area has been voluntarily contracted immediately above the ground stories, with a preference for going high rather than spreading out. It is such works that have emboldened imagination to conceive a city with lance-like towers set in open plots of greenery. Such an extreme will doubtless never be attained, but it augurs that many new visions still lie hidden in the future.

Although the modeling of masses has thus absorbed the chief interest, the surfaces remain

MASSES

Hotel Shelton, New York

MASS AND LINE
The American Radiator Building, New York

and must have their treatment. Of late there is a tendency to abandon the plane enveloping curtain of McKim, and again to energize the effect with aspiring lines. Raymond Hood led the way in this with his American Radiator Building, which embodies also so many other tendencies of the time: the early contraction of the tower to permit windows all about, the solicitude for variety of mass evident in the octagonal suggestion of the beveled corners and in the complex stepping of the upper stages, the interest in color. The black piers leap upward, tipped with gold, the golden crown blazes in the level sun and gleams afar at night.

When the *Chicago Tribune* set a great prize for the design which should surpass all others, projects came from every country. Vertical emphasis predominated. Hood and Howells, adjudged the winners, in repeating and varying the motive of the Radiator Building, took a step backward by closely following the details of Gothic. The second prize fell to a Finn, Eliel Saarinen, who, for his square tower with simple receding bastions, evolved a ribbed mantle of striking originality. Sullivan hailed it, in his dying breath, as a Phœnix from the ashes of his old hopes. The artist has found little opportunity to realize his poetic dream, although plagiarists have been quick to turn it into prose.

Meanwhile other inspired works have been rising. The vast bulk of the Telephone Building looms on New York's water-front. The architects, McKenzie, Voorhees and Gmelin, have given their designer, Ralph Walker, free play. Here, as in Corbett's studies, is an effort to fill the maximum legal mass, subject to the requirements of light and the suggestions of steel construction. A multitude of cubical steppings and recessings make the transition from the block below to the vast square tower with its receding summit. Trivial reminiscences of the Gothic have fallen away; puerile suggestions of historic style no longer mar the interior. As in the best German work, all is smelted anew in the creative spirit.

It is in these buildings, particularly in the Shelton, that we see the larger unity of American modernism, toward the poles of which—functional expressiveness and abstract form—its masters have variously striven. In Sullivan's quest of expression he did not lose simplicity of mass. His tall buildings are crystalline, cast in one jet, like those of McKim and Platt. In spite of the difference of their superficial markings, vertical or horizontal, they are essentially at one. So too, in the upbuilding of the new colossi of steel we see the balanced and centralized mode which McKim had brought again to honor in low buildings of masonry. Scarcely one of the new giants has a corner tower, not one has the romantic, unbalanced massing which was universal in the day of Richardson, and which might equally—but for the power of the new classic tradition—have ruled to-day. In all the welter of experiment, the basic character of our modern work—its measured simplicity and breadth, above all, its clarity—has remained in common.

XVI

MANHATTAN

Photograph by Sigurd Fischer, courtesy of McKenzie, Voorhees, and Gmelin

MASS AND LINE

The New York Telephone Building

Courtesy of K. Lonberg-Holm

THE GROTESQUE
Times Square at Night

CHAPTER XVI

MANHATTAN

ON THE narrow island of Manhattan, the heart of New York, titanic forces have built the great city of the present.

Little more than a generation ago, when the centenary of the Constitution was celebrated on the site of Federal Hall, Wall Street was but the dingily pretentious image of a conventional street in any third-rate European capital, the town was a shabby overgrown Bloomsbury. Looking at the mock châteaux of Fifth Avenue, Henry James could liken New York to "an ample child-less mother, who consoles herself for her own sterility by an unbridled course of adoption."

Almost overnight, by the natural richness of a new continent exploited with mad energy by man and machine, this city has become the center of the world, the center of commerce, of finance, of power. A wild growth has sprung suddenly to the gigantic, surpassing every inherited measure, grotesque in its assertive individualism, in its contrast with survivals of the old. Its first qualities are heightened dimension, heightened contrast, heightened insistence, heightened energy. Houses rise suddenly to fifty stories, among forlorn doomed relics of faded Victorian gentility. East and west at a single corner we pass from the degraded tenements, half emptied by prosperity, to vast new hotels, offices and apartment-palaces. On Broadway the endless firework of flaming signs leaps and flashes above the torrent of traffic, the whirlpool of pleasure. All is exaggerated, still unordered, but intoxicating, already full of fantastic beauty.

In the midst of this anarchy certain buildings isolate themselves by their own unity and power. Their value lies not merely in dimension, but in form. In spite of their variety they have much in common. There are the beginnings of a style.

Where rebuilding has progressed furthest the grotesque aspects tend to vanish, a larger coherence is visible. Not consciously designed, it is none the less real. Down-town, economic forces have built in a great pyramid, culminating over the costliest sites. A vast man-made mountain

Photograph by the Publishers Photo Service

The Magic Mountain—Lower Manhattan from the Bay

From "Manhattan, the Magical Island," courtesy of Ben Judah Lubschez

THE CANYON
Lower Broadway

rises from the sea, cleft in its heart by the canyon of Broadway. At night a fairy city of light floats above the rivers, barred by the mighty arcs of their great bridges.

Already, within the city, as Keyserling has felt, turmoil and haste begin to give place to peace and leisure. The crude expedients of youth begin to disappear, the noise diminishes. Men are learning to master their great creature, to find room and time again for contemplation and for the practise of the gentler arts.

All over the land the vision of Manhattan has captured the imagination. Chicago restlessly struggles to outrival New York itself. Philadelphia is building its own great pyramid about the tower of City Hall. Detroit, making in a year many times more cars than the number of its inhabitants, dreams of the highest tower of all, soon to be a reality. In little cities of the West rise buildings which, laid flat, would reach into the open prairie. The spell of the metropolis is on them all.

The traveler from across the sea is dazzled by the apparition, as in the days when the pilgrim from distant Hungary abased himself before the spires and beneath the vaults of Chartres and Amiens. Like him, too, he may aspire to go and do likewise. But the French Gothic, however admired, was never fully understood far beyond the borders of the Ile-de France, and was imitated timidly and with concessions fatal to its full effect. It is doubtful if the world may ever see, outside America, another Manhattan.

Every great achievement in building, pushed to its extreme by the élan of its creators, has in it something of the monstrous, from which those who have not gone along step by step will recoil. Even at home the evolution outruns its own causes and advantages; its own protagonists are aghast at the final result. Already the drawbacks are apparent, and limiting forces begin to operate. It has not been too soon. Above the waters stands the magic mountain of steel and stone, shining and glorious, as one of the crowns of human endeavor.

EPILOGUE

EPILOGUE

ARTISTIC creation is a never-ending stream. In art, unlike science, there is no single "right" way. Only to stand still is wrong, for that belies the imaginative and creative nature of art itself. What is modern for one generation is no longer modern for the next. We may admire the apt epigram of our fathers' time, but if we persist in repeating it, it becomes a platitude to-day. Art must change to live.

In the revaluing which accompanies every such change of ideals, many a reputation will go down. The little men will have only a historical significance. The quality of greatness is to survive such changes, by fulfilling the new demands as well as the old. Among the American architects are more than one who give promise of living on, not merely as the founders of great schools of the past, but as masters who can speak out of the past in the eternal language of form.

Which way is forward at the moment will be known only from the grand march of events.

EPILOGUE

The architect can not act alone, he must be in step with his brothers in life and in every art; but he may have his great part in establishing the direction and carrying his fellows with him. Whither the march may turn is not determined only by material factors. The soul of man is master.

The path lies in darkness, but as the light dawns behind, it will be seen that great deeds have been done along the way.

THE END

NOTES

NOTES

This book is based primarily on the writer's published researches on single topics, which have been freely laid under contribution, with the consent of the publishers, in the text.

Few attempts have hitherto been made to discuss the history of American architecture as a whole, either by itself or as part of a general study of American art. Talbot F. Hamlin's *The American Spirit of Architecture* (1926) is a rich collection of illustrations with brief interpretive and critical text. Lewis Mumford's *Sticks and Stones: a Study of American Architecture and Civilization* (1924) has its emphasis on the second term of the subtitle. Jacques Gréber's *L'architecture aux États-Unis: preuve de la force d' expansion du génie francais*, 2 vols. (1920) is mainly a study of contemporary types, and emphasizes particularly the French contribution, studied also in Louis Réau's *L'art francais aux États-Unis* (1926). Werner Hegemann and Elbert Peets' *Amerikanische Architektur and Stadtbaukunst* (1925), adapted from the same authors' *American Vitruvius: an Architect's Handbook of Civic Art* (1922), is concerned chiefly with the problems of formal, spatial design.*

---

*Since this manuscript was in the publisher's hands there has appeared Thomas E. Tallmadge's *The Story of Architecture in America*, New York, Norton (1927). It is of independent value only in its discussion of the Chicago school of 1880 and onward, on which it gives some important material.

NOTES

COLONIAL PERIOD AND EARLY REPUBLIC

For the Colonial period and the early republic a very full bibliography has been published by Richard F. Bach in the Architectural Record, vol. LIX (1926), pp. 265 ff.

Here are given only certain references amplifying or illustrating the discussion in this book:

General

WILLIAM ROTCH WARE, ed: *The Georgian Period*, in *American Architect*, 1898-1902. A corpus of early measured drawings and pioneer discussions.

KIMBALL: *Architecture in the History of the Colonies and of the Republic*, in *American Historical Review*, vol. XXVI (1921), pp. 47-57, has discussion of the relation between European and early American work, especially primitive shelters and churches.

Public Works

KIMBALL: *Jefferson and the First Monument of the Classical Revival in America* (the Virginia Capitol), 1915.

KIMBALL: *The Origin of the Plan of Washington* in *Architectural Review*, vol. VII (1918), pp. 41-45.

ELBERT PEETS: *The Genealogy of L'Enfant's Washington* in *Journal of the American Institute of Architects*, vol. XV (1927) pp. 115, 151, 187.

GLENN BROWN: *History of the United States Capitol*, 2 vols. Washington, Government Printing Office, 1900-1903.

NOTES

Documentary History of the United States Capitol, Washington Government Printing Office, 1904.

KIMBALL and WELLS BENNETT: *The Competition for the Federal Buildings, 1792-93* in *Journal of the American Institute of Architects,* vols. VII-VIII (1919-20).

WELLS BENNETT: *Stephen Hallet and his Designs for the National Capitol, ib.,* vol. IV (1916), pp. 290, 324, 376, 411.

KIMBALL and BENNETT: *William Thornton and his Designs for the National Capitol,* in *Art Studies,* vol. I (1923) pp. 76-92.

History of Public Buildings under the Control of the Treasury Department, Washington, Government Printing Office, 1901.

The Diary of John McComb, Jr. in *American Architect,* vol. XCIII, (1908), p. 15.

The Original Plans of the City Hall, New York, ib., pp. 43-46.

MONTGOMERY SCHUYLER: *The New York City Hall,* in *Architectural Record,* vol. XXIII (1908), pp. 387-390.

EDWARD S. WILDE: *John McComb, Jr. Architect,* in *American Architect,* vol. XCIV, pp. 49-53, 57-63.

I. N. PHELPS STOKES: *The Iconography of Manhattan Island,* vol. I, (1916), pp. 454-456, 460-467 (on Joseph Mangin).

C. C. MAY: *The New York City Hall,* in *Architectural Record,* vol. XXXIX (1916), pp. 309, 474, 513.

NOTES

KIMBALL: *The Genesis of Jefferson's Plan for the University of Virginia*, in *Architecture*, vol. XLVIII (1923), pp. 397-399.

KIMBALL: *Jefferson the Architect* (The University of Virginia), in *Forum*, vol. LXXXV (1926), pp. 926-931.

KIMBALL: *The Bank of Pennsylvania*, in *Architectural Record*, vol. XLIV (1918), pp. 132-139.

KIMBALL: *The Bank of the United States, 1818-1824*, in *Architectural Record*, vol. LVIII (1925), pp. 581-594.

EDWARD BIDDLE: *Girard College*, in *Proceedings of the Numismatic and Antiquarian Society of Philadelphia*, vol. XXVIII (1919), pp. 199-215.

Churches

AYMAR EMBURY II: *Early American Churches*, New York, Doubleday, 1914.

C. A. PLACE: *From Meeting House to Church in New England*, in *Old-Time New England*, vols. XIII, XIV (1923), pp. 149, 3.

KIMBALL: *Latrobe's Designs for the Cathedral of Baltimore*, in *Architectural Record*, vol. XLII (1917), p. 540, LIII (1918), p. 37.

Domestic Architecture

KIMBALL: *Domestic Architecture of the American Colonies and of the Early Republic*, New York, Scribner's, 1922.

[234]

NOTES

J. E. CHANDLER: *The Colonial House*, New York, Mc-Bride, Winston, 1916.

LEIGH FRENCH: *Colonial Interiors*, New York, Helburn, 1923.

HOWARD MAJOR: *Domestic Architecture of the Early American Republic: The Greek Revival*, Philadelphia, Lippincott, 1926.

H. C. MERCER: *The Origin of Log Houses in the United States*, in Bucks County Historical Society Papers, vol. V (1924).

For works dealing with single regions see the topographical list.

Regional works

A wealth of local variety is shown in the numbers of the *White Pine Series of Architectural Monographs*, New York, 1915 to date.

New England

D. MILLAR: *Measured Drawings of Some Colonial and Georgian Houses*, 2 vols., New York, Architectural Book Publishing Company, 1916 ff.

R. C. KINGMAN: *New England Georgian Architecture*, New York, *ib.*, 1913 (measured drawings).

J. M. CORNER and E. E. SODERHOLZ: *Domestic Colonial Architecture in New England*, Boston, 1891 (large photographs).

NORMAN M. ISHAM and A. F. BROWN: *Early Rhode Island Houses*, 1895, and *Early Connecticut Houses*, 1900, Providence, Preston & Rounds Company.

[235]

NOTES

The pioneer discussions of the evolution of the early frame house.

B. C. TROWBRIDGE, ed. *Old Houses of Connecticut*, New Haven, Yale University Press, 1924.

J. F. KELLY: *Early Connecticut Architecture*, New York, Helburn, 1924 (measured drawings), and *Early Domestic Architecture of Connecticut*, New Haven, Yale University Press, 1924.

New York region

AYMAR EMBURY II: *The Dutch Colonial House*, New York, McBride, 1913.

H. D. EBERLEIN: *Manors and Historic Homes of the Hudson Valley*, Philadelphia, Lippincott, 1924.

W. J. MILLS: *Historic Houses of New Jersey*, Philadelphia, Lippincott, 1903.

Philadelphia region

THOMPSON WESTCOTT: *The Historic Mansions and Buildings of Philadelphia*, Philadelphia, Porter & Coates, 1877.

H. C. WISE and H. F. BEIDLEMAN: *Colonial Architecture in Pennsylvania, New Jersey, and Delaware*, Philadelphia, Lippincott, 1913.

H. D. EBERLEIN: *Colonial Homes of Philadelphia and its Neighborhood*, Philadelphia, *ib.*, 1912.

A. L. KOCHER: *Early Architecture of Pennsylvania*, in *Architectural Record*, vol. XLVIII (1920), p. 513; XLIX (1921), pp. 31, 135, 233, 311, 409, 519; L,

NOTES

pp. 27, 147, 215, 398, LI (1922) p. 507, LII, pp. 121, 435.

Chesapeake region

J. E. CHANDLER: *Colonial Architecture of Maryland, Pennsylvania and Virginia*, Boston, 1882 (large photographs).

J. M. CORNER and E. SODERHOLZ: *Domestic Colonial Architecture in Maryland and Virginia*, Boston, Boston Architectural Club, 1892 (large photographs).

L. A. COFFIN and A. C. HOLDEN: *Brick Architecture of the Colonial Period in Maryland and Virginia*, New York, Architectural Book Publishing Company, 1919.

PAUL WILSTACH: *Potomac Landings*, New York, Doubleday, 1921.

J. M. HAMMOND: *Colonial Mansions of Maryland and Delaware*, Philadelphia, Lippincott, 1914.

H. F. CUNNINGHAM and others: *Measured Drawings of Georgian Architecture in the District of Columbia*, New York, Architectural Book Publishing Company, 1914.

R. A. LANCASTER: *Historic Virginia Homes and Churches*, Philadelphia, Lippincott, 1915.

Southeastern region

E. R. DENMARK: *Architecture of the Old South*, Atlanta, The Southern Architect and Building News, 1926.

NOTES

Huger Smith: *Dwelling Houses of Charleston*, Philadelphia, Lippincott, 1917.

Albert Simons and Samuel Lapham: *Charleston*, New York, American Institute of Architects, 1927.

E. A. Crane and E. Soderholz: *Examples of Colonial Architecture in Charleston and Savannah*, Boston, Boston Architectural Club, 1895, (large photographs).

Southwestern region

Cleve Hallenbeck: *Spanish Missions of the Old Southwest*, New York, Doubleday, 1926.

Rexford Newcomb: *Franciscan Mission Architecture of Alta California*, New York, Architectural Book Publishing Company, 1916 (measured drawings), and *The Old Mission Churches and Historic Houses of California*, Philadelphia, Lippincott, 1925.

L. B. Prince: *Spanish Mission Churches of New Mexico*, Cedar Rapids, Torch Press, 1915.

Biographical

Joseph Jackson: *Early Philadelphia Architects and Engineers*, Philadelphia, 1923.

Kimball: *The Colonial Amateurs and their Models: Peter Harrison*, in *Architecture*, vol. LIII (1926), pp. 185, 209.

Lambeth and Manning: *Jefferson as an Architect*, Boston, Houghton Mifflin, 1913.

Kimball: *Thomas Jefferson, Architect*, 1916.

J. J. Jusserand: "Mayor L'Enfant and the Federal City" in his *With Americans of Past and Present Days*, New York, Scribner's, 1916.

[238]

NOTES

GLENN BROWN: *The Octagon* (Thornton), American Institute of Architects, n. d.

E. S. BULFINCH: *The Life and Letters of Charles Bulfinch*, Boston, Houghton Mifflin, 1896.

C. A. PLACE: *Charles Bulfinch: Architect and Citizen*, Boston, Houghton Mifflin, 1925.

B. H. LATROBE: *The Journal of Latrobe*, New York, Appleton, 1905.

E. L. GILLIAMS: *A Pioneer American Architect* (Strickland) in *Architectural Record*, vol. XXIII (1908), p. 135.

For further references on Thornton, Hallet, and the other competitors for the Federal Buildings see under *Public Works* above. There are documented biographical sketches of American architects by the present writer and others in the volumes of Thieme-Becker's *Allgemeines Künstlerlexikon* and the *Dictionary of American Biography*.

SINCE THE CIVIL WAR

The chief source here is the file of journals, particularly the *American Architect* from 1876, the *Inland Architect* from 1881, the *Architectural Review* from 1890, the *Architectural Record* from 1892, the *Brickbuilder* and *Architectural Forum* from 1892, *Architecture* from 1900.

ROYAL CORTISSOZ: *Leaders in American Architecture* in his *Art and Common Sense*, New York, Scribner's, 1913.

NOTES

Marianna Griswold Van Rensselaer: *Henry Hobson Richardson*, Boston, Houghton Mifflin, 1888.

Montgomery Schuyler: *The Works of Richard Morris Hunt*, in *Architectural Record*, vol. V (1895) p. 97.

John V. Van Pelt: *A Monograph of the William K. Vanderbilt House*, New York, the Author, 1925 (with biography of Richard Morris Hunt).

Obituary of William Le Baron Jenney, in *Architectural Record*, vol. XXII (1907), pp. 155-157.

Harriet Monroe: *John Wellborn Root*, Boston, Houghton Mifflin, 1896.

Louis H. Sullivan: *The High Building Artistically Considered*, in *Lippincott's Magazine*, March, 1896.

Louis H. Sullivan: *The Autobiography of an Idea*, New York, American Institute of Architects, 1924.

Louis H. Sullivan: *A System of Architectural Ornament*, New York, *ib.*, 1925.

Kimball: *Louis Sullivan*, in *Architectural Record*, vol. LVII (1925), pp. 289-304.

Alfred Hoyt Granger: *Charles Follen McKim*, Boston, Houghton Mifflin, 1913.

Lawrence Grant White: *Sketches and Designs of Stanford White*, New York, Architectural Book Publishing Company, 1920.

A Monograph of the work of McKim, Mead and White, 4 vols. folio, New York, Architectural Book Publishing Company, 1915.

[240]

NOTES

GLENN BROWN: *Personal Recollections of Charles Follen McKim*, in *Architectural Record*, vol. XXXVIII (1915), pp. 575, 681; XXXIX (1916), p. 84.

KIMBALL: *What is Modern Architecture?* in *Nation*, vol. CXIX (1924), p. 128.

THOMAS HASTINGS: Letter in *American Architect*, vol. XCIV (1909), pp. 3-4.

The Works of Carrère & Hastings, in *Architectural Record*, vol. XXVII (1910), pp. 1-120.

CHARLES MOORE: *Daniel H. Burnham*, Boston, Houghton Mifflin, 1921.

D. H. BURNHAM and F. D. MILLET: *World's Columbian Exposition, The Book of the Builders*, Chicago, Columbian Memorial Pub. Soc., 1894.

PETER B. WIGHT: *Daniel Hudson Burnham and his Associates*, in *Architectural Record*, vol. XXXVIII (1915), p. 1.

GLENN BROWN: *Artistic Growth of the Washington Plan*, in *Architectural Record*, vol. LIX (1926), pp. 311, 424, 571.

A Monograph of the Work of Charles A. Platt, New York, Architectural Book Publishing Company, 1913.

The Architecture of John Russell Pope, New York, Helburn, 1924.

Portraits of Ten Country Houses designed by Delano and Aldrich, New York, Doubleday, 1921.

NOTES

Competition for the New York Court House MCMXIII, New York, Architectural Book Publishing Company, n. d.

F. M. DAY and others, ed: *American Country Houses of Today*, 5 vols., New York, Paul Wenzel, 1912-1926.

FRANK LLOYD WRIGHT: *Sketches and Executed Work*, 1912.

H. TH. WIEDEFELD and others: *Wendingen: Frank Lloyd Wright*, Stantpoort, C. A. Mees, 1925. (Here are included Wright's first three papers, *In the Cause of Architecture*. Others are appearing currently in the *Architectural Record*.)

H. DE VRIES: *Frank Lloyd Wright*, 1926.

C. H. WHITAKER and others: *Bertram Grosvener Goodhue*, New York, American Institute of Architects, 1925.

The Tribune Tower Competition, Chicago, 1923.

B. J. LUBSCHEZ: *Manhattan, the Magical Island*, New York, American Institute of Architects, 1927.

Among the records of recent foreign visitors the following may be particularly mentioned:

ERICH MENDELSOHN: *Amerika: Bilderbuch eines Architekten*, Berlin, Rudolf Mosse, 1926. Also his paper in the *New York Times Magazine*, August 22, 1926.

ELIE FAURE: *America and Rome* in *New York Times Magazine*, July 17, 1927.

[242]

NOTES

JOHNNY ROOSVAL: *America, New Found Land of Art*, in *New York Times Magazine*, September 7, 1924.

On the work of the last generation, observed through a score of years with a view to writing its story, not a little has been gained from personal acquaintance and conversation with many of its masters, living and dead, with McKim and Mead, Cram and Day, Sullivan and Wright, Wilby and Corbett, and their associates and helpers. With Paul Cret, D. Everett Waid, Royal Cortissoz and Clarence Stein, among many others, I recall more than one stimulating discussion. To all of these I owe my heartiest acknowledgments.

INDEX

INDEX

Buildings in general are listed under the name of the town where they stand, except plantation houses and other buildings in isolated rural situations, which are under their own names.

The entries for American architects carry their dates, where exactly ascertainable.

Academic architecture, 35, 42, 46, 70-71

Adam style, 52, 87-90

Adshead, S. D., 185

Adobe, 206

Æsop's Fables, 51

Albany, N. Y., 89
  Van Rensselaer manor-house, 47

Albro, Lewis C., 207

Alcove beds, 86

Aldrich, Chester H. (1871-   ), 178

Alexandria, Va., Masonic Memorial, 205

Altars, 64, 76

American Academy in Rome, 187

American Academy of Art and Letters, 187

American influence abroad, 116, 185-186, 196, 198, 199-200

Ampthill, Va., 91

Andalusia, Pa., 104

Annapolis, 52
  Brice house, 51
  Chase house, 47

Apartment buildings, 184-185

Arcade, 44, 46, 65

Arches, 49, 50, 89, 125, 165
  triumphal, 77, 100

Architects, amateur, 42-43, 44, 45, 80, 81, 106

Architects, professional, 43, 80, 97, 106

Art nouveau, 199, 210

Arts and Crafts movement, 128

Arizona, 63

Arlington, Virginia, 103

Ashmont, Mass., All Saints' Church, 131

Athens, Erechtheum, 96
  Parthenon, 96, 98-99, 104
  Monument of Lysicrates, 100
  Temple on the Illissus, 102
  Theseum, 99

Athens, Ga., 105

Atkinson, Robert, 185

Attwood, Charles (1849-95), 168

Auvergne, 125

Bach, J. S., 160

Bacon, Henry (1866-1924), 181

INDEX

Bacon's Castle, Va., 31
Balconies, 65, 105, 122
Baltimore, Cathedral (Catholic), 101
  Cathedral (Episcopal), 132
  Chapel of St. Mary, 113
  Homewood, 90
  Washington Monument, 100
Balusters, 50, 59, 89
Banks, 95-96, 98-100, 113, 124, 178, 182, 191
Barboursville, Va., 91
Barns, 59
Baroque architecture, 42, 64
Basilicas, 46, 206
Beaujour, Major, 96
Behrens, Peter, 199
Belcher, John, 186
Belfries, 45, 63, 64, 65
Belmead, Va., 114
Benjamin, Asher, 89
Bennington, Vt., church, 75
Bergen sandstone, 59
Berks County, Pa., 59
Berlin, 199
  Einsteinturm, 200
Bernard, Sir Francis, (1711-79) 43
Berry Hill, Va., 104
Biddle, Nicholas, 97, 100, 104
Biltmore, N. C., 127
Beverly, Mass., Browne's Folly, 31
Blakely, John, 96
Blockhouses, 20
Blois, 127
Bodley, G. F., 130
Books, influence of, 42, 71
Borie, Charles, 210

Boston, 41, 77, 89
  Beacon monument, 77
  Bunker Hill Monument, 100
  Christ Church, 37
  Faneuil Hall, 43, 46
  Hancock house, 47, 50, 58
  King's Chapel, 44
  Mason house, 87
  Museum of Fine Arts, 124
  Old South Church, 37, 45
  Old State House, 44
  Otis house, 86
  Post Office, 120
  Province house, 31
  Public Library, 164-165
  St. Paul's church, 102
  Sergeant house, 31
  State House, 78
  Swan house, 87
  Trinity Church, 125
  Washington arch, 77
Brackets, 36, 50, 64, 122
Bremo, Va., 91
Brick, 22-24, 37, 46, 122, 128, 129, 139, 193
  importation of, 23-24
  sun dried, 21
Brickmaking, 24, 122
Bridgeport, Conn., Iranistan, 120
Bridges, 135, 141
Brown, Joseph, 45
Brownstone, 164
Bruce, James Coles, 104
Brunel, Marc Isambard, (1769-1849) 85
Bryn Mawr College, 129
Buffalo, Guaranty (Prudential) Building, 191-192

INDEX

Buffalo—*con't.*
Larkin Building, 194
Bulfinch, Charles, (1763-1844)
77, 85, 87, 89, 178
Burnham, Daniel H u d s o n,
(1846-1912), 152-53, 166,
168, 174, 176, 206
Burr, Aaron, 49
Burwell, Carter, 43
Buttresses, 64, 65
Byron, 112
Byzantine style, 204

California, 64, 207
Cambridge, Mass., 104
Christ Church, 44
Harvard College, early build-
ings, 37, 43
Memorial Hall, 124
Canberra, 198
Cape Cod, 57-58
Capitols, colonial, 45-46
Federal, 78-82, 97
state, 73, 76, 77-78, 208
Carpenter's Company, Phila-
delphia, 42, 44
Carrère, John M., (1858-1911),
129
Carpeaux, 159
Casements, 22, 27, 30, 35, 128
Cast-iron, 122, 138, 139, 144
"Cat-and-clay," 21, 22, 59
"Caves," 19
Cedar, 21
Ceilings, coved, 50
plaster, 51
ornamented, 88
Cement, 140
Cèzanne, 160, 200

Charleston, S. C., 90, 113
Miles Brewton house, 48-49,
50, 51
Robert Brewton house, 36
Huger house, 51
Pinckney house, 48
Nathaniel Russell house, 87
St. Michael's, 44
St. Philip's, 44
Charlestown, Mass., 21
Joseph Barrell house, 87
Charlottesville, Va., C h r i s t
Church, 102
University of Virginia, 83-84,
91, 178-79
Châteaux, 127, 161, 221
Chesapeake Bay, 90
Chicago, 151-59, 176, 192, 198-
99, 223
fire, 143
Auditorium, 155
Field warehouse, 126, 155
Home Insurance Building,
143
Hull house, 192
Tacoma Building, 144
Tribune Building, 215
Winslow house, 193
World's Fair, 165-168
Chimayo, N. M., 64
Chimneys, 57, 60, 127, 128
brick, 17
catted, 22
clustered, 27, 31
stone, 23
Chimneypieces, 36, 42, 50
Chippendale style, 42, 51
Christ Church, L a n c a s t e r
County, Va., 37

[249]

INDEX

Churches, 19, 28-30, 37, 43-45, 63-65, 101-02, 124, 129, 131-32, 195-96

Circular buildings, 181
  houses, 106-07
  rooms, 86-87

City halls, 31, 45, 82

Clapboards, 58

Classic revival, 71-107

Clay, 17, 19, 24, 63, 65; mortar, 23

Cleveland, O., Leader-News Building, 185

Cloisters, 65

Colleges, 37, 82-84, 126, 129, 178-179

Colonial architecture, 17-66
  revival, 129, 161, 206-07

Colonnades, 80, 83, 91, 100, 167, 178, 179, 180, 207

Columbia, S. C., 76; Capitol, 77

Columns, 44, 47, 48-49, 50, 72, 73, 82, 95, 98, 103, 104, 105
  triumphal, 77, 100

Commission of Fine Arts, 187

Composition ornament, 89-90

Concrete, 135, 140, 195-197

Connecticut, 19

Connecticut Valley, 45, 58

Constable, John, 112

Cooper, James Fenimore, 105, 114

Cope, Walter, (1860-1902), 129

Copley, John Singleton, 58

Corbett, Harvey W., (1873-), 186, 205, 211

Cornices, 36, 89

Cornish, N. H., gardens, 177

Courbet, 159

Craftsmanship, 128, 130-131

Cram, Ralph Adams, (1863-), 130, 131

Crescent, 89

Cupboards, 50

Danvers, Mass., Hooper house, 48

Darwin, Charles, 148, 153

Davis, Alexander Jackson, (1803-1892), 99, 102, 113, 114

Day, Frank Miles, (1861-1918), 129

Delacroix, 112

Delano, William A., (1874-), 178

Delaware valley, 20

Department stores, 138

Detroit, 223
  Ford factory, 197

Domes, 64, 80-82, 83, 101, 102, 179, 180

Doorways, 36, 41, 42, 47, 49, 50, 58, 88

Dormers, 59

Downing, Andrew Jackson, 114, 173

Drayton's Palace, S. C., 48

Dressing-rooms, 85

Dublin, Custom House, 77
  Leinster House, 80
  Royal Exchange, 77, 85
  Wellington Monument, 100

Dunkards, 59

Dutch Colonial, 58, 206

Dutch colonists, 17, 58

INDEX

E-plan, 31

East, 151, 165, 166-167

East Barsham, 114

Eastlake, C. L., 128

École des Beaux-Arts, 125, 126, 149, 154, 161, 165, 166, 171-172

Eclecticism, 119-32, 204-06

Edenton, N. C., St. Paul's, 37

Edinburgh, National Monument, 99

Edgehill, Va., 91

Egyptian architecture, 102

Einstein, Albert, 200

Elevators, 142

Elizabethan style, 27, 31, 129

Elliptical rooms, 86-87

Emerson, Ralph Waldo, 125

Endecott, John, 21

Engineering, 198

English colonists, 17, 20

"English cottage style," 114

English influence, 19, 20-22, 28, 31, 35, 37, 41-46, 50, 51, 52, 75, 77, 80, 87-88, 90, 91, 111, 114, 115, 123-24, 128, 130, 132

"English wigwams," 19

Ephrata, Pa., 59

Erie Canal, 105

Evolution, theory of, 148, 150

Eyre, Wilson, (1858-   ), 129

Expositions, London, (1851), 138

   Philadelphia Centennial, 128

   Chicago World's Fair, (1893), 165-168, 185

   Paris, (1900), 185

   Paris, (1925), 210

Expression, theory of, 148-150

Factories, 135, 136, 141, 194-95, 196-97, 199

Faience, 139

Fairfield, Va., 31

Fanlights, 49, 89

Farmhouses, 57-60

Farmington, Conn., 45

Farmington, Va., 91

Federal period, 69ff.

Fireplace, 30, 36, 50, 193

   See also Chimneypieces, mantels

Fireproofing, 139, 155, 158

Flaubert, 159

Florida, 129, 207

Formalism, 159-160, 162, 163, 167, 171-187, 195, 203-205, 212-217

Forts, log, 20

Fowler, Orson Squire, 106

Fox, Samuel M., 96

"Frail houses," 17

Franciscans, 64

Frankfort, Ky., capitol, 99

Fredericksburg, Kenmore, 52

Freehold, N. J., Tennent Church, 37

French colonies, 63, 65

French influence, 42, 51, 72, 76, 77, 78, 81, 82, 85-86, 91, 106, 120, 125-27, 171-72, 206

Frets, 51

Frontiersmen, 20

Fulton, Robert, 136

Functionalism, 148-150, 155-158, 159, 183, 191, 193-200

Furness, Frank, 125

INDEX

Gardens, formal, 177
Gables, 128
Garden temples, 112
Gables, 31, 36, 48, 49, 50, 58, 60, 65
    stepped, 31
"Garrisons," 20
Georgetown, D. C., Tudor Place, 90
Georgia, 20
Georgian architecture, 36, 41-53
Germans in America, 20, 21, 59, 123

German influence, 29, 208, 209
German Renaissance style, 123
Germantown, Pa., 59
    Cliveden, 47
Gibbs, James, 44, 75, 80
Gilbert, Cass, (1859-   ), 184
Gilmor, Robert, 113
Glass, 17, 22, 122-123, 197
    leaded, 27, 30, 35
    plate, 138
Glen Cove, L. I., Manor House, 177
Goethe, 130, 147, 192
Godefroi, Maximilian (c. 1760-1833), 112
Goodhue, Bertram G., (1869-1924), 130-132, 207, 208, 209
Gothic style, 27-29, 35, 150, 184, 205
    Chippendale, 51
    collegiate, 129-130
    Italian, 124
    Victorian, 124, 125

Gothic revival, 111-16, 124, 130-32
Governors, colonial, 20-21, 43, 48, 49
Gréber, Jacques, 172
Greco, 160
Greece, 98
Greek cross, 101
Greek revival, 74, 95-107
Greek War of Independence, 103, 105
Griffin, Walter Burley, 198
Guadet, Julien, 165
Gulf states, 63, 105

H-plan, 31
Hadfield, George, (d. 1826), 97, 103
Hallet, Stephen, 80, 82, 97
Half-timber, 20, 21, 128
Hamilton, Alexander, 85, 87, 136
Hamilton, Andrew, (1676-1741), 45
Hankar, Paul, 199
Harrison, Peter, (1716-1775), 43, 44, 46
Harmon, Arthur Loomis, 213
"Harvard brick," 129
Harvard College,
    early buildings, 37, 43
    Memorial Hall, 124
Haviland, John, (1793-1852), 116
Hastings, Thomas, (1860-   ), 129
Herder, 147
Hingham, Mass., "Old Ship" meeting-house, 29

INDEX

Hoban, James, (c. 1762-1831), 77, 87

Hoadley, David, (1774-1839), 89

Holabird, William, (1854-   ), 144

Hood, 59

Hood, Raymond, (1881-   ), 215

Hooker, Philip, (1766-1836), 89

Hope Lodge, Horsham, Pa., 36

Horta, Victor, 199

Hotels, 129

Houses, 17, 19-22, 27, 30-31, 46-53, 85-91, 102-07, 112-15, 177-78, 193-94
  brick, 20, 31
  frame, 20-21, 22, 27, 30-31
  half-timbered, 20-21
  stone, 20
  log, 19-20
  palisaded, 19
  plans, 35, 47, 85-87

Howe, Lord, 48

Howells, John Meade, (1868-   ), 215

Hudson valley, 41, 58

Hugo, Victor, 112

Hunt, Richard Morris, (1827-95), 126-127

Hurley, N. Y., 58

Ibsen, 159

Impressionists, 159

Indians, 19, 63, 64

Ingres, 160

Industrialism, 122-123, 131, 135-141, 151, 153

Iron, 135, 138, 141-144, 151
  cast, 122

Ironwork, 65

Irving, Washington, 105, 113

Italian gardens, 177
  Gothic, 124

"Italian villas," 120

Jacobean architecture, 27, 31

Jails, log, 20

James, Henry, 221

James, John, 43

Jamestown, first houses, 19
  church, 28

Jefferson, Thomas, (1743-1826), 37, 43, 49, 70, 71, 74, 76, 77, 79, 80, 83, 86, 91, 95, 97, 102, 103, 106, 107, 112, 116, 175

Jenney, William Le Baron, (1832-1907), 143-144

Jesuits, 63-64

Jones, Inigo, 41-42, 50

Kahn, Albert, (1869-   ), 196

Kahn, Ely Jacques, (1884-   ), 214

Kansas City, Mo., 152
  War Memorial, 207

Karlsruhe, 78

Kearsley, John, (1684-1722), 44

Keats, John, 148

Kent, William, 111

Kentucky, 105

Klauder, Charles Z., (1872-   ), 129

Laguna, N. M., Chapel of San José, 63

INDEX

Lake Forest, Ill., McCormick house, 177

Lake Geneva, Wis., Bartlett house, 192

Lancaster County, Pa., 59

Landscape gardening, 111, 114

Latrobe, Benjamin Henry, (1766-1820), 95-98, 101, 106, 112, 113, 116, 136, 178

Lebanon County, Pa., 59

Ledge stone, 23, 129

Lemoulnier, 120

L'Enfant, Pierre Charles, (1754-1825), 76, 78, 79, 88, 136, 173-74

Lenox, Mass., church, 75

Libraries, 81, 126, 164-65, 179

Lime, 23

Lincoln, Neb., capitol, 208

Lindeberg, Harrie T, 207

Liverpool, cathedral, 132

Log houses, 19-20

London, Bush House, 186
  churches, 44
  Crystal Palace, 138
  Great Fire, 23, 35
  Manchester House, 88
  Somerset House, 46
  Wellington Monument, 100

Long Island, 58

Louis XIV style, 51, 78

Louis XV style, 51, 76, 85, 86, 88

Louisiana, 206

Lowell, Guy, (1870-1926), 180

Luther, Martin, 29

Lutyens, Sir E. L., 186

MacBean, 44

McComb, John, (1763-1853), 82, 89

Machine age, 122-23, 194, 199, 221

McIntire, Samuel, (1757-1811), 89

McKenzie, Voorhees & Gmelin, 216

McKim, Charles Follen, (1847-1909), 160-61, 164-165, 167, 168, 174, 175, 178, 179, 181, 186-187, 204, 215, 217

McKim, Mead & White, 128, 160-165, 171, 173, 184

Magonigle, H. Van Buren, (1867-   ), 207, 208

Mangin, Joseph, 82, 116

Mansard roof, 120

Mantels, 50, 51, 89

Marble, 95
  chimneypieces, 50

Maryland, 41

Masonry, 22, 27, 155

Masonic temples, 113, 180

Massachusetts Bay colony, 18

Mausoleum, 180

Mead, William Rutherford, (1846-   ), 161

Medford, Mass., Royall house, 47-48

Medieval survivals, 27-28
  revival, 111-116

Medway, S. C., 31

Meeting-houses, 29-30, 45

Meigs, Arthur, (1882-   ), 207

Mendelsohn, Erich, 200

INDEX

Middleton, S. C., 31

Middletown, Conn., 58

Mill construction, 141

Millbach, Pa., Muller house, 59

Milledgeville, Ga., 113

Mills, Robert (1781-1855), 74, 97, 100, 101, 113, 178, 179

Missions, 63-65

Mississippi river, 65

Modernism, 147-217

Monet, 159

Monier, Joseph, 140

Monticello, Va., 49, 86, 91

Montpelier, Va., 91

Monuments, 79, 100-101, 207-208

Moorish style, 119, 167

Morris, William, 128, 130

Mount Airy, Va., 47

Mount Vernon, Va., 88

Mulberry, S. C., 31

Museums, 124, 138

Musée Napoleon, 97

Nantucket, Mass., 58, 105

Napoleon, 74, 102

Napoleon III, 125

Nature, influence of, 130, 148, 152, 153-154, 157-158, 159, 192, 193

Neo-classicism, 162-165, 166-168, 171-187, 203-207, 217

New Bedford, Mass., 105

New England, 19, 20, 23, 47, 50, 89, 129, 206

churches, 28, 29

farmhouses, 57-58

New France, 19, 65

New Haven, Conn., 89

Capitol, 99

Yale College, 37

New Jersey, 19, 58

churches, 29

New London, Conn., Eastover, 177

New Mexico, 63, 206

New Netherlands, 19, 24

New Orleans, 65-66

New Palz, N. Y., 58

New Spain, 19, 63-65

New York, 41, 58, 59, 89, 113, 143, 160, 206, 211-17, 221-24

American Radiator Building, 215

apartment buildings, 184-185

John Jacob Astor house, 127

Broadway, 222, 223

Bush Building, 205, 214

Cathedral of St. John the Divine, 206

Century Club, 164

City Hall, 82

Colonnade Row, 105

Columbia University, 179

Court House, 180-181

Custom House, 99

Federal Hall, 76, 77, 221

Federal Reserve Bank, 185

Fifth Avenue, 221

Fraternity Clubs, 214

French Chapel, 102

Garment Center, 212

Gerry house, 127

Grace Church, 115

Grand Central Station, 183

The Grange (Hamilton), 87

INDEX

New York—*con't.*

Madison Square Garden, 164

Madison Square Presbyterian Church, 179

Merchants' Exchange, 100, 178

Metropolitan Life Building, 212

Roger Morris (Jumel) house, 49

Municipal Building, 184, 214

National Academy of Design, 124

National City Bank, 178

New York University, 113, 179

New York Telephone Building, 216

office buildings, 183-85, 211-16, 222

Old City Hall, 31, 45, 76

Old Post Office, 120

Old Trinity Church, 29

One Fifth Avenue, 205

Park Avenue, 176, 214

Park Theatre, 85

Pennsylvania Station, 183

Post Office, 178

prison, 116

Prison Ship Martyrs' Monument, 178

Ritz Tower, 214

St. Bartholomew's, 131

St. Patrick's, 115

St. Paul's Chapel, 44, 76

St. Vincent Ferrer, 132

Shelton Hotel, 213, 214, 216

Singer Building, 212

Trinity Church, 115

New York—*con't.*

Vanderbilt, William K., house, 127

Villard houses, 164

Wall Street, 221

Washington Arch, 178

Woolworth Building, 184

World Building, 143

Newels, 50-51

Newport, R. I., 43

Casino, 128

"cottages," 127

Market, 46

Redwood Library, 46

Synagogue, 44

Nîmes, Maison Carrée, 72, 73

Norfolk, Va., Barton Myers house, 90

Northwest, 105

Oak, 21, 31

Oak Park, Ill., Unity Temple, 195-196

Obelisks, 100-101

Octagonal form, 47; houses, 106; rooms, 86

Office buildings, 135, 142-44, 153, 155-59, 183-85, 191-92, 211-16, 222

Olmsted, F. L., Jr., 174

Orders, 48, 112

Outbuildings, 60

Overhang, 30, 58

Owen, Robert Dale, 114

Oxford movement, 130

Pæstum, Temple at, 103

Palisaded houses, 19

Palladio, 43, 70, 71, 106

style of, 42, 71

INDEX

Paneling, 36, 37, 50, 59

Pantries, 86

Farris, Alexander, (1781-1852), 89

Patios, 65

Pavilions, 48

Paris, 72, 77

  Bibliothèque Ste. Geneviève, 165

  Exposition of 1925, 210

  Garde-meuble, 78, 79

  Hôtel de Salm, 72, 79, 91

  Hôtel de Ville, 120

  Louvre, 79, 120

  Madeleine, 74

  Place de la Concorde, 78

Paterson, N. J., 136

Penn, William, 35; house, Philadelphia, 36

Pennsylvania, 21, 23, 59, 129, 206

Peristyles, 100, 104, 180, 181

Perkins, D. H., (1867-), 192

Pews, 30

Philadelphia, 41, 51, 113, 129, 223

  Bank of Pennsylvania, 95, 96

  Bank of Philadelphia, 113

  Bank of the United States, 85

  2nd Bank of the United States, 98, 99

  Belmont, 51

  Bingham house, 86, 88

  Carpenter's Company, 42, 44

  Cedar Grove, 36

  Christ Church, 44, 46

Philadelphia—con't.

  Centennial Exposition, English building, 128

  Eastern Penitentiary, 116

  Fidelity Mutual Building, 210

  First shelters, 19

  Girard College, 100

  Independence Hall, 45

  Lansdowne, 49

  Lemon Hill, 87

  Library, 81

  Merchant's Exchange, 100

  Morris "folly," 88-89

  Mount Pleasant, 47, 48

  Museum of Art, 177, 210

  Old Post Office, 120

  Parkway, 176

  Pennsylvania Academy of the Fine Arts, 97-98, 124, 125

  Powel house, 52

  President's House, 88

  John Reynolds (Morris) house, 75

  Sedgeley, 112

  Solitude, 88

  State House, 45

  Stenton, 36

  University of Pennsylvania, 129

  Water Works, 106, 136

  Woodlands, 87, 88

  see also Germantown

Philippines, 176

Piazzas, 58

Piedmont, 91, 206

Pilasters, 41, 44, 45, 46, 47, 49, 50, 58, 89

[257]

INDEX

Pine, 30

Pittsburgh, Pa., Calvary Church, 131

Plantation houses, 60, 104, 114-15

Platt, Charles A., (1861-), 177, 185-217

Plymouth Colony, 19, 57-58

Pond, I. K., (1857-), 192

Poore, Ben Perley, 129

Pope, John Russell, (1874-), 178, 180

Poplar Forest, Va., 106

Porticoes, 36, 41, 44, 45, 46, 48-49, 72, 73, 76, 83-84, 88, 91, 95, 98, 101, 104, 180

Portland, Me., 89

Portsmouth, N. H., 41, 129
    McPhaedris house, 36

Post-colonial work, 75

Power houses, 197, 199

"Prairie style," 198

Primitive shelters, 17-20

Princeton University, 129, 130

Prisons, 115-116, 126
    log, 20

Providence Plantation, 23

Providence, R. I., Joseph Brown house, 75
    First Baptist Church, 45

Provincial types, 57-66, 128-29

Public buildings, 41, 45-46, 69, 72-74, 76-82, 97-101, 175, 178, 211

Pugin, Augustus Welby, 115, 149, 150

Put-in-Bay, O., Perry Memorial, 178

Queen Anne movement, 128, 161

Radnor, Pa., St. David's, 29

Railway stations, 135, 140-41, 182-83

Ramée, Joseph, (d. 1842), 84, 100

Rancho Camulos, Cal., 65

Realism, 159

Red House, Bexley Heath, 128

Regensburg, Walhalla, 99

Renaissance, 27-28
    Italian, 149, 164
    German, 123

Renwick, James, 114, 115, 130

Republican period, 69ff.

Rhode Island, 23

Richards, Charles R., 210

Richardson, A. E., 185

Richardson, Henry Hobson, (1838-86), 125-126, 130, 155, 161, 166, 217

Richmond, H. P., 181

Richmond, Va., 72, 76
    Capitol, 73, 74, 79
    Monumental Church, 102
    Penitentiary, 116

Riverside, Ill., Coonley house, 194

Roche, Martin, 144

Rodin, 159

Roman influence, 71-72

Romanticism, 111-116, 124, 125, 130, 161, 196, 208

Romanesque style, 114, 125-126, 166, 167, 204, 205, 213

Rome, 77
    Cancellaria, 164

INDEX

Rome—*con't.*
  Colosseum, 46
  Pantheon, 83, 84
  Mausoleum of Hadrian, 181
Roofs, 21, 27, 28, 35, 57-60, 63,
    65, 114, 127, 193; gam-
    brel, 36, 59; mansard,
    120
Root, John Wellborn, (1887-),
    152, 153, 155, 166
Rosewell, Va., 48
Rough-cast, 128
Roxbury, Mass., Shirley house,
    48
Ruskin, John, 13, 123, 125, 130,
    149, 150, 185
Russia, 107
Rustication, 47, 65, 82

Saarinen, Eliel, 215
Salem, Mass., 21, 41, 89, 129
  Derby Mansion, 89
Salons, 86-87
St. Augustine, Fla., Cathedral,
    63
  Governor's House, 63
St. Gaudens, Augustus, 174, 177
St. Louis, Wainwright Build-
    ing, 156-59, 191-92
  Wainwright mausoleum, 191
St. Luke's, Isle of Wight Coun-
    ty, Va., 28
St. Petersburg, 78
San Antonio, Tex., Missions, 64
San Diego, Cal., Mission, 64
  Estudillo house, 65
San Francisco, 176
  Mission, 64
San Gabriel, Cal., 65

San Juan Capistrano, Cal., 65
San Xavier del Bac, Arizona,
    64
Santa Bárbara, Cal.,
    Mission, 65
  De la Guerra house, 65
Santa Fé, N. M., Palace, 65
Sash windows, 36
Sawmills, 22
Savannah, Ga., 113
Saxe-Weimar, Bernhard, von,
    98
Schenectady, N. Y., Union Col-
    lege, 84
Schuylkill valley, 23
Science, influence of, 147-148,
    194
Scotland, 107
Scott, Sir Gilbert, 132
Scott, Sir Walter, 112
Scroll-saw, 122
Secession, 199
Sedding, J. D., 130
Semper, Gottfried, 150, 152
Set-backs, 211
Shaw, Howard Van D., (1869-
    1926), 192
Shaw, Norman, 128, 186
Shellwork, 51, 52
Sheathing, 31, 36, 128
Shingles, 21, 37, 58, 59
Shirley, Va., 36
Shops, 138
Short Hills, N. J., Casino, 128
Shutters, 22
Side-lights, 89
Skylights, 138

INDEX

Sky-scrapers, 142-44, 183-85, 200, 203, 205, 211-17, 221-24

Slate, 21

Smibert, John, (1688-1751), 43

Smith, Robert, (d. 1777), 44

Sod, 17

South, 60, 88, 91, 113

South Carolina, 31, 41

Southwest, 65

Spanish colonial, 129, 131, 206-07

Spanish Colonies, 63-65

Spatial form, 47, 86-87, 101, 179, 182-83

Spotswood, Alexander, 43

Springfield, Mass., civic group, 205

Spring Green, Wis., Taliesin, 194

Stairs, 46, 47, 50, 82, 86, 87

State houses, 45-46, 73, 77-78

Staunton Hill, Va., 114-115

Steel, 135, 139, 142, 144, 155, 159, 166, 167, 183, 184, 185, 191, 211, 213
    sash, 197

Steeples, 21, 44, 45

Stewardson, John, (1858-1898), 129

Stone, 22-23, 58, 59, 60, 129

Stratford, Va., 31

Strawberry Hill, 111

Strickland, William, (1787-1854), 97, 98, 100, 113

Stucco, 59, 114

Sullivan, Louis, (1856-1924), 125, 142, 152, 153-159, 167, 183, 185, 191-192, 200, 215, 216

Surveyor of the Public Buildings, 97

Swan-neck, 42

Swedish colonists, 17, 20

Swiss colonists, 20

Symmetry, 30

Tabernacles, 50

Tarrytown, N. Y., Sunnyside, 113

Temple, imitation of, 72-74, 80, 83-84, 91, 95-96, 98-100, 102-106, 114, 180, 181

Terra cotta, 139, 158

Tessé, Comtesse de, 72

Texas, 63

Thatch, 17, 21-22

Theatres, 85

Thomaston, Me., Henry Knox house, 87

Thornton, William, (1759-1828), 81, 89, 90, 96, 97

Tidewater region, 24, 41

Tile, 21, 65

Timber, abundance of, 17, 22

Tokio, Imperial Hotel, 196

Tolstoi, 159

Towers, 44, 64, 114, 125, 211-17

Town, Ithiel, 99, 100

Town halls, 126

Town planning, 76, 78, 173-77

Tracery, 29

Trappe, Pa., Muhlenberg's church, 29-30

Triumphal arch, 77, 100
    column 77, 100

Tryon, Governor, 43

Tuckahoe, Va., 31

Tucker, George, 98

Tudor style, 129

[260]

INDEX

Union College, 84

University of Pennsylvania, 129

University of Virginia, 83-84, 91, 178-179

Universities, *see also* Colleges

Upjohn, Richard, (1802-78), 115

Valois, style of, 127

Van Brunt, Henry, 152

Vaults, 64, 113, 182

Versailles, 78

Victorian style, 122, 175
Gothic, 124, 125

Vienna, 199, 210

Villa Rotonda type, 72, 80, 106

Viollet-le-Duc, 149, 150-151, 152

Virginia, 23, 28, 41, 73, 206

Wagner, Otto, 199

Wagner, Richard, 159

Wainscot, 31

Walker, Ralph T., 216

Walter, Thomas U., (1804-1888), 100

Walpole, Horace, 111

Waltham, Mass., Gore house, 87
Lyman house, 87

Washington, George, 88

Washington, D. C., 76, 78-82
Capitol, 79, 81, 97, 100, 122
Cathedral, 206
Lincoln Memorial, 174-75, 181-82
Mall, 78
National Academy of Sciences, 200

Washington, D. C.—*con't.*
Octagon, 90
Park Commission Plan, 173-76
President's House, *see* White House
St. John's, 101
Smithsonian Institution, 114
State Department, 120
Temple of the Scottish Rite, 180
Treasury, 100, 178
Washington Monument, 173-74
White House, 78, 79-80, 87, 91, 175

Watertown, Mass., Oakley, 87

Wattle, 17, 19

Weather-boards, 21, 30

Webster, Noah, 70

Wellford, Robert, 90

Wells, Joseph Morrill, 161-162

Welsh, 29, 59

West, 151-159, 165, 166-67, 198

West Newbury, Mass., Indian Hill, 129

West Point, N. Y., Military Academy, 131

Westover, Va., 47, 51

White, Stanford, (1853-1906), 161, 164, 178, 179-180, 205

Whitehall, Md., 47

Whitewash, 58, 63

Whitman, Walt, 160

Wigwams, English, 19

Wilby, Ernest, 196, 198

William and Mary College, 37

Williams, Roger, 23

INDEX

Williamsburg, Va., B r u t o n Church, 37, 43

Capitol, 45

Governor's Palace, 72

William and Mary College, 37

Wilton, Double Cube, 50

Windows, 17, 22, 36, 47-48, 50, 64, 65, 122-23, 197

casement, 22, 27, 30, 35, 128

Palladian, 41

sash, 36

Winthrop, John, 18, 21

Wren, Sir Christopher, 37, 42, 44, 186

Wright, Frank Lloyd, (1869-), 192-196, 198-199, 200

Yale College, 37, 130

Yonkers, N. Y., Philipse Manor, 52

Zantzinger, Clarence, (1872-), 210

Zola, 159

Zoning law, 211-12